FOWLER'S MOON

FOWLER'S MOON

by

NIGEL THORNYCROFT

Illustrations
by
CORONA

Coch-y-Bonddu Books
2010

To Rods
who shared the thrills
and so doubled them.

FOWLER'S MOON
BY NIGEL THORNYCROFT
Illustrated by Corona Thornycroft

Copyright © estate of Nigel Thornycroft

First published by John Sherratt & Son, Altrincham, 1955
This edition © Coch-y-Bonddu Books Ltd, Machynlleth, 2010
New Introduction © Phil Gray 2010

ISBN 978 1 904784 27 2

Also published in a limited hardback edition

Coch-y-Bonddu Books Ltd, Machynlleth, Powys SY20 8DG
01654 702837

Printed and bound in Great Britain by TJ International Ltd

INTRODUCTION

More than half a century has passed since the first edition of this book was published in 1955 and it is certainly that long since I bought my copy. The fact that the coastal marshes described in the book were the very same that muddied my own thigh boots between the 1960s and 80s led to a correspondence with the author, Nigel Thornycroft, and subsequently with his widow, Corona. I regard it as an immense privilege to have been asked to write this Introduction, and do so as a tribute to my old friends.

Nigel's story, and that of Corona, who so beautifully illustrated this book, is told more fully in their biography, *Nigel and Corona*, subtitled *A family story of adventure, sport, wilderness and war from England to Africa*, which is to be published simultaneously with this volume.

The Thornycrofts had moved to Southern Rhodesia after the Second World War, where they farmed a sizable acreage of tobacco and maize. Nigel was a blood relative of the famous 'Mad Jack' Mytton and shared some of that gentleman's eccentricity; the first time he came to stay with us, he pulled out a polythene bag containing at least three pounds of his own tobacco from which to roll up a cigarette!

Our correspondence covered many years until Nigel's death, during which we swapped news mainly of a sporting nature, but his letters contained much on their life in Southern Rhodesia and in particular on their war, culminating in the coming into being of the new state of Zimbabwe.

Fowler's Moon was surreptitiously drafted on a roll of toilet paper with a stub of pencil while Nigel was, as he put it, a guest of the Gestapo. He had escaped twice from POW camps and for his efforts was placed in solitary confinement. He told me he came out more or less horizontal, but by filling his mind with memories of marshes, widgeon and geese he had preserved his sanity.

Fowler's Moon is the best wildfowling book I have ever read. Illustrated by Corona's evocative scraperboard sketches, it tells the story of a young man's introduction to the sport of wildfowling. Following his adventures though the season, it is written so that the reader is there with him, crouching in a creek as the geese approach, or under the moon with the thrill of widgeon calling all around. More than once within the text there are poignant thoughts expressed that neatly sum up the very essence of wildfowling.

"The book describes how a novice wildfowler, Rory, the narrator, learns wildfowling lore and practice from a more experienced friend, a silver fox farmer called William. It is entirely typical of Nigel that he narrates the story from the point of view of the novice, when in real life he was the more experienced William. Rory is probably based on his Cambridge friend Roderick (Rods) Parkyn, who later married Nigel's sister Puss and to whom the book is dedicated. John Humphreys described Nigel's style as modest but thrilling. There are few rhetorical flourishes but you cannot doubt that every incident actually happened to Nigel on the ground and in the conditions that he describes with telling detail. He had experienced the wet and the cold, felt the frustrations redeemed by occasional triumphs and thrilled to the beauty of the fens and the shoreline, and the birds that scrape a living from them. There cannot be many first time authors who could have resisted the temptation to finish the tale of a wildfowler's journey with a triumphant right and left at geese. Nigel's fictional alter ego fumbles his final stalk, misses with both barrels and suffers a furious self-recrimination that strikes a chord immediately with those who have been there." (David Thornycroft in *Nigel and Corona*).

Fifty years on, some things in the book are naturally a bit dated, but when our hero's mentor complains of the cost of eight-bore cartridges at sixpence each, it all adds to the fun of it and does not detract from the book at all. The scene, the fowl and the methods are much the same as ever they were. The list of quarry species was longer in those days, with a large range of waders plentiful and available to harvest, and the season for duck began in August. Despite these greater opportunities, Nigel preached, and practiced, restraint and common sense. It is largely through such an example that we are still able to practice our sport on the coasts and fens of Britain, and that our wildfowl and wetland bird populations remain healthy. The wild geese of the winter now visit our shores in greater numbers than ever before, and we still thrill to the whistle of the widgeon under the moon. So, sink into an armchair, open the pages, smell the tang of the foreshore and hear the incoming tide whisper as it slides stealthily, almost sinisterly, over the mud.

Phil Gray
Oundle
East Northamptonshire

Phil Gray is the author of four wildfowling books, including The Washlanders *(1990) and* Fenland Fowler *(2001). A long-time friend and protégé of Nigel Thornycroft, Phil modelled his own book,* Fowler's Footsteps *(2007) on* Fowler's Moon. *In his third book,* Fenman in Africa *(2006), he describes his relationship with the Thornycrofts and in doing so, provides the reader with a stepping stone between* Fowler's Moon *and* Nigel and Corona.

Gray read Fowler's Moon *in 1959, with its stories of wildfowling in his native coastal marshes. This prompted him to write to the author, by that time farming in Rhodesia, and a warm friendship and sustained correspondence arose.* Fenman in Africa *quotes from the Gray-Thornycroft letters, discussing wildfowling, punt-gunning with Sir Peter Scott, the last days of Ian Smith's Republic of Rhodesia and the early years of Robert Mugabe's Zimbabwe. The book includes hunting with the Thornycrofts on the Zambezi as well as selections and illustrations from Corona Thornycroft's game diaries which describe her own exploits wildfowling, game shooting and fishing.*

AUTHOR'S FOREWORD

The aim of any book should, I am told, be to stimulate the interest of the reader with a view either to his instruction or diversion.

There is, I fear, little enough of instruction in these pages. A beginner may glean a grain or two, but there is not much for the fowler of experience. No one should gain in local knowledge, for place names and pinpoint localities I have been at some pains to distort. That at least I owe to the birds who have given and shown me so much.

But each and every flight and event portrayed took place under the weather conditions and at the time of year and phase of moon and tide I have described. Few are in any way extraordinary; and since there is nothing new under the sun—or moon—and fowl are within fixed limits surprisingly conservative in their reactions, I have little doubt that precisely similar adventures have occurred to scores and hundreds of other fowlers. Yet to these I hope this book may still give pleasure, not through the second-hand absorption of my little thrills, but by stirring some chord leading to personal and private memories—the only sort worth having.

"Yes, it was on just such a night—" and presently the book will fall unheeded, its aim accomplished, while in the fire grow skeins and troops and companies, and the air seems full of music.

There is my hope.

And now, since the merit of a preface has always appeared to me to lie in its brevity, let me at least claim that for virtue.

June 1955

Merryhill,
Marandellas,
Southern Rhodesia.

1

Looking back, the more I think of it the more unbelievably lucky does that chance encounter seem. London in August is never at its best. This August it was even more sultry and smelly than usual, and I had succeeded in working myself up into a fine state of gloom over the beastliness of a life which forced me to work therein to keep body and soul together when all I really wanted was to be out in the open country, breathing in air that was fit to breathe, with a gun or a rod, or even a pair of glasses in my hand. Even the spare time I had, my all-too-short week-ends, it swallowed up, simply because I could not yet afford to pass them in the way I longed to. Here was another shooting season just beginning, as barren of promise—for me—as its predecessors. I had, in short, wrought myself into a notable state of self-pity—and then I met William.

Not that I looked upon that meeting at the time in any way as the solution of my troubles; an hour's relief at most, perhaps. He was sitting at a table in the restaurant where I usually lunched, because it was the nearest to the office, and I hailed him joyfully.

Now William had been my greatest friend at school. We had arrived together, moved up together step by step, played the same games together, and spent as much of our holidays in each other's homes as possible. We'd both lived in the country all our lives; our youthful horizons had been bounded by a world of birds and beasts and flies and cartridges, and our one idea, when we grew old enough— and in consequence, rich enough—had been to acquire neighbouring estates, and every year take moors or forests which adjoined each other, and run our shoots and moors and forests as shoots and moors and forests had never been run before or since, till they were the envy of all who saw them.

Alas for our dreams! When we left school William had gone on to Cambridge, while I had slipped straight into the family business and been shipped off abroad for three long years; and although to begin with we had kept up a more or less sporadic correspondence, this had gradually died a natural death as we began to find our feet in the rush and scurry of life. William, I knew, lived somewhere in the country, but how or where, I'd very little notion; and I suspect his knowledge of my movements was equally vague. My job, I suppose, was a good one as such jobs go. It clothed and fed me, and my future was pretty well assured; but meanwhile, I missed the old country life most damnably, and felt at times that I'd sell my soul to be out and away from all the rush and bustle of the city, alone with a rod or gun in my hand.

That lunch was a cheerful meal, but all too short, for William had to rush off to keep a date with some excessively boring-sounding individual, which was the sole reason he'd come up to town. I did, however, persuade him to forswear his original intention of taking the night train home and agree to spend it in my flat; although he assured me he would not be there until late.

He wasn't; and it was nearly ten o'clock by the time we'd finished dinner, too late for anything but a quiet evening.

It was very pleasant sitting chatting in the firelight opposite William once again. He'd altered surprisingly little during the last five years—a bit broader perhaps, and the lines of his face a little more mature, but he looked as hard and lean as ever—and there was the same quiet twinkle in his eye as there always used to be when we faced each other across the study table, after a day spent bird-nesting or trying to tickle old Colonel Culver's trout. No diffidence, no awkward moments; somehow we picked up the threads, just where we'd let them fall five years before.

I suppose, during dinner, I must have been rather airing my opinion of town life in general, and my town life in particular, for when we'd got comfortably settled down William remarked:

"You know, Rory, I'm not sure you aren't making a bit of an error about the cost of amusing yourself in the country! Depends on the lines you're thinking along, of course—if your head's still full of grouse moors and covert shoots and salmon rivers it is pretty impossible, I admit; but there's the hell of a lot of quiet fun to be had for next to nothing even these days, if you're prepared to look for it. I've modified my ideas considerably since the old days—"

"Ye-es—if you live among it, I suppose there must be a certain amount of sport going begging. But I haven't the time to find it. I've tried staying at various pubs that advertised shooting and fishing—very good value some of them are, too—but it always costs me about double what I'd expected by the time I've finished! One day, I suppose, I`ll have enough brass to be able to afford it all!"

"That's not quite what I'm getting at, old son. You're heading for the finished article all the time, and by the time you're able to afford that, you'll probably be too old and venerable to enjoy it. Besides, you're a foreigner playing in the country only, and as such liable to be stung by the inhabitants. All the same, if you're not too proud, there are a lot of unconsidered trifles in the way of sport to be picked up. Pigeons, shooting on the foreshore, coarse fishing, and so forth; but they all take learning, or you'll get nothing—except the fun of being out."

William paused for a while, then continued: "I told you I'd started a small silver fox farm when I came down, because I decided I couldn't face the thought of a job in a town. I have to do most of the work on it myself, and at times it's meant pretty hard scratching to make ends meet. Livestock are the hell of a tie, I've discovered—this, incidentally, is the first night I've been away since Christmas —but I do get quite a lot of spare time in bits and pieces, especially in the autumn and winter, which is my slackest time. It means having to look for my amusements pretty close to my doorstep, but its extraordinary what a lot there are; I'm even getting together the nucleus of a small rough shoot. It's not everybody's meat, I suppose, but I'd not swap it for any job in a town at a thousand pounds a year!"

After that, the conversation turned on people and places we both had known, and all too soon it was time for bed. I lay awake for a long time thinking over what William had said. It did sound an intriguing existence. That foreshore shooting—I must find out more about that from him before he left.

But at breakfast next morning, William forestalled me.

"Look here, Rory, I've got a suggestion to put to you. If you really are as hard up for somewhere to go over the weekends as you make out, I've got a spare bed that's very much at your disposal, and you know I'd love to have you just whenever you like. Only I live very very quietly, and I'd maybe not be able to spare the time to play the perfect host. If you care to use it as a sort of headquarters, though, we'd get quite a lot of time together and I dare say we'd manage to amuse ourselves. Think it over, anyway, and come down on Saturday if you've nothing better on."

Think it over! I didn't need much time for that—and on Saturday, as it happened, I'd a date that could easily be put off. One snag I found, though, when I came to look them up, and that was trains. William lived down in Norfolk, just where the flat rich fenlands broke up into the sandy carrstone of the "high" land, and I found that even if I left the office at midday, I couldn't get down there till nearly four o'clock. Returning was easier, though it meant getting up at a pretty godless hour on Monday morning. Still, it was feasible.

Then I had a brain wave. Tentatively I suggested to my uncle, who ran the office, that if I worked on alternate Saturdays till six o'clock, and took the week-ends in between from Friday night, I should not be defrauding the firm of my valuable time; and rather to my surprise he seemed inclined to agree that, under the circumstances, something of the sort might be arranged. Here was progress. I found myself longing for Saturday and really getting something fixed.

2

AUGUST 20

It was a sultry hot August afternoon when William met me at the little station, and I chucked my baggage into the back of a motor so battered and so patched about that it was well-nigh impossible to tell how long ago or by whom it had been built. But it went: noisily and smellily and importantly, it went. It had a personality of its own, that motor, and in time I grew nearly as attached to it as William was. After a couple of miles of panting up and down dusty winding lanes, whose hedges guarded stubbles and the green squares of roots with here and there a field of clover, we swung down to a level plain of grass that was cut and cut again by a pattern of little dykes; then up a steep and very home-made drive, and here was William's home. A pair of cottages built out of old brown carr, and moss grown tiles their roof. William had bought them both, and knocked them into one without destroying in the least their outside symmetry. Inside it was blissfully cool after the dusty glare of the August sun.

"Mrs. Timms will show you your room, Rory—I must fly and feed the beasts—see you in half an hour,"—and William was gone.

A dear old body of a housekeeper took me in charge, and presently I found myself in a tiny whitewashed bed room under the eaves, looking out over a flat green checkerboard of fen which stretched away a mile or more to a built-up double dyke that wormed its way across my front into the level distance to the right. At a corner, where the dyke turned from me, a gleam of silver showed the river that it held. Beyond, the land reached flat again, then gradually rose to a horizon of firs and birch and clumps of big old oaks, from the midst of one of which peeped the roof and grey stone tower of a village church. But whereas the checkerboard this side of the river was varying shades of green—green grazed by cattle, freshly cut for hay, or waving dark in patches of old rush—beyond, it was mainly golden stubble in far larger squares, with occasional big patches of a duller, darker, shade of green that were potatoes growing.

The cottage stood halfway up the slope where the land ridged steeply up from the fen, in a sea of broom and gorse that grew where the carrstone thrust too near the surface to allow of cultivation. It must have been a glory two months ago, but now only a stray golden bloom remained aflaunt against the sombre green. To the left, the slopes gradually closed in on either side of the valley till the winding river dykes were hidden by scattered tree clumps growing down towards them.

Behind the house, as I later learnt—behind where William kept his "beasts"—the hill sloped up to a table of light and sandy arable. Poor soil enough for cultivation, but most excellent for partridges, with here and there a hollow filled with broom and gorse and twisted thorns.

Little enough signs of habitation. A few scattered cottages along the near fen edge where the road was and, beyond the river, a solitary farm-house with attendant barns and ricks.

Of such was William's kingdom. Quiet, he had threatened. It was the kind of quiet that I could take a lot of; pure bliss after the rush and smells of London town. Idly I wondered where his "nucleus of a rough shoot" lay. Those fens looked as if they might hold a snipe or two in winter, or a stray cock pheasant or a hare among the rushes; maybe in hard weather even odd duck and teal along the dykes? A shout from below roused me. "Come on, Juliet, when you've finished gazing out of the window, I want my tea."

This the admirable Mrs. Timms produced in an alcove curtained off from the main living room, which William had created by stripping half the ground floor of one cottage till a single ceiling reached from wall to wall, with two great beams that ran across its whitewashed breadth. Beyond the curtain an open red-brick hearth confronted two cavernous armchairs and, flanking it, reaching from floor to ceiling, was an old-fashioned glass-fronted gun case, with cupboards underneath for cartridges and such: while opposite, the wall was taken by a built-in bookcase, stuffed full to overflowing. A comfortable, lived-in sort of room.

Behind the glass of the gun cupboard gleamed as pleasing an array of glossy blue-black barrels as you could wish to see. There was "Fanny", an enormous 8-bore chambered to take 4-inch shells; a workmanlike non-ejector 12-bore magnum—not so glossy this—the salt and mud of many flights had worn off all the blueing; a lovely 12-bore game gun by a famous maker, which I coveted at sight; a double .410; a very nice little Mauser magazine .22 with a wide cut V and a big back-sloping platinum bead of a foresight; and tucked away in a corner a long-barrelled .22 pistol, also by a German firm, whose muzzle—whisper it —was screw-cut to take a silencer. A miscellaneous collection of rods hung along the back of the cupboard to complete a picture that fairly made my mouth water. Tentatively I cast my fly

"Rather a lot of guns you've got there, William?" and William rose to it.

"I suppose they are a fairly formidable-looking array," he answered—rather complacently, I thought, "but I'd hate to be without any of 'em. They've each got their pet particular use, and each one saves the other, or me, unnecessary wear and tear. Except 'Fanny'—she's a bit of a vanity, I admit. But I suddenly came across her ridiculously cheap after the most maddeningly barren week when night after night I'd been watching geese stream in across the face of the moon well out of magnum range. And I fell. I thought she'd maybe throw some sort of a pattern with AA's which'd reach 'em. She does too; I've killed geese with her that I'd never have fired at with a magnum. But to be honest I'm not sure that I haven't missed as many close-up ones that I'd have probably got with a magnum, not to mention chances at odd duck and widgeon. She weighs eighteen pounds, you see, and her shells cost me sixpence-halfpenny a time, so I have to think twice before

I loose her off. She doesn't kick though, not one bit," running his hand over the beautifully polished stock with the air of one condoning the naughtiness of a favourite child. "All the same, she's a bit of a white elephant, I'm afraid. I don't take her out very often nowadays.

"A magnum I think you must have if you're going to do any fowling on this coast. At least, what is essential is that you have a rough-and-ready weapon of some sort, and don't take down your best game gun. Mud and blood and sand and salt is a mixture that'll take the bloom off a gun quicker than anything I know, and you can't spare 'em that. That's a thing you'll have to get this winter if you're coming down with me, and it's a game I think you'll love unless you've changed a lot.

"The others? Well, the four-ten is useful spring and summer when you don't want to lug a heavy gun around, and also for odd days rabbiting in cover. It's partly laziness, I admit, but it does come in when my others are away having their annual overhaul. That," pointing to the 12- bore, "is the beauty who does most of my shooting for me; I picked her up second-hand. I'd like a pair, but that's a pipe-dream which'll have to wait.

"We'll give the two-two a little exercise presently if you like. She's a pleasant job with as sweet a trigger-pull as you'll meet in a long day's walk. I was very lucky to pick her up, and to my mind that bolt action is infinitely preferable to any automatic in this sandy soil. There's so much less to go wrong. The sights I fitted later. They're useless on a range, but wait till you try them on a bunny in open country in the half-light. That sloping bead collects the reflection of the sky like a mirror.

"The pistol has its uses too—"William stopped suddenly, and stared at me, hard. "Blast you, Rory, I believe you deliberately tried to get me wound up!"

A providential scratching at the door saved me the trouble of an answer.

"Hullo, there's Bill—I suspect he's been to see a lady-friend in the village or he'd have been here when you arrived. I do bar having to keep him shut up by day—"

He opened the door to let in a liver and tan spaniel—at least, the new arrival was more like a spaniel than any other breed that I could think of. Nevertheless, an attractive hound; there was plenty of breadth between those friendly eyes, and later I had good cause to marvel at his working powers.

Presently William took me round to see the foxes. As he explained, they weren't attractive at this time of the year, as the old ones had shed their coats and the cubs had reached the leggy, lanky stage. All of them, young and old alike, were just black thin-coated foxes, and showed little signs of the glorious fur they would carry in another month or two. And then I met Harry, last but not least of William's ménage. Ostensibly, Harry helped look after the foxes and did odd jobs. In fact he did, and more, for he looked upon the foxes as his own and took a fitting pride in them. In addition to that and the thousand-and-one odd jobs that kept on cropping up, he spent most of his spare time in keepering William's little shoot. Fixed working hours he had none, but he did about twice as much as any man I've ever met when work was needed. William and he were far more partners than master and man, and Harry's loyalty was absolute. I thought, and still think, that William was very lucky in his servants.

By the time we had finished seeing round, and satisfied the thirst that this engendered, it was time for supper.

"We might slip down to the fen afterwards if you like, sometimes the odd duck comes in to one or other of the dykes of an evening to help wash down its cropful if its been feeding on the stubbles. Or we might take the rifle and try for a bun?"

I plumped for the fen, and the chance of a duck, however remote

The sun was dropping into a haze of pink as we sauntered down. Bill, who was hunting a little ahead, put up a barren pair of partridges, and I watched them as they fled across the fen till they dwindled and vanished, then reappeared for a second as they braked with the whole length of their backs towards us, and dropped in to the grass.

"Funny how few ever rear a family successfully down here," William remarked. "They come down late on though, after the rush seeds, and some always stay and try!"

At a place where two six-foot dykes met, William left me, and himself went a hundred yards or so beyond and sat down on the dyke-edge. Already the sun had dropped below the flat horizon, and a faint pearly mist was rising to hang like a veil a few feet above the level of the grass. The heat and drought of the day was over, and a blessed freshness was seeping into the air. The scents of meadow sweet and new-mown hay contested as to which should rule the senses. Two bats, big fellows, appeared from nowhere and started hawking insects up and down the dykes and over the meadows, and a vole dived into the water with a soft plop almost at my feet. From the high ground behind the cottage I could hear a partridge creaking a good-night roll-call of her brood before they finally settled down. I fairly revelled in the peace and quiet of it all. Over the meadow ahead a white owl was a-hunting, quartering the ground back and forth, back and forth only a few inches above the grass tops on wings as silent as the night itself.

Then out of the last red glow of sunset three specks appeared—steadying out of the dancing horde of insects above the dyke. Swiftly they grew. Three duck, and flying low towards us.

Here was the object of our evening, coming fast. But they passed just out of range, their wings a-whisper—and almost I was glad of it. The spell of this night was too perfect to be shattered by any nitro blast.

A half-hour more we sat here, till the last of the reflected sunlight faded from the sky, and the stars came slowly out, and the mist thickened into a dense white curtain sealing in the fen and us below it. A rustle at my elbow, and there was Bill, with William close behind.

When I looked out of my bedroom window late that night there was no fen, only a soft white sea that stretched into infinity with here and there a treetop straggling black above it.

Next day I began to appreciate a little of what William had meant when he talked of livestock being "a hell of a tie." Harry was away early, and soon after we had finished cleaning out, one of the cubs started throwing fits. By the time that was sorted out, it was time to prepare their evening feed, then to give it, and with one or two other little routine jobs it was supper time. They were graceful beasts, those foxes, even in what William called the "naked stage", and the orange tawny eyes set in black masks with a powdering of silver across the brows, were undeniably handsome.

Between whiles we settled many little points as well. William was delighted with my alternate week-end scheme, but agreed to my keeping an old pushbike at the station so that my comings and goings should leave him independent. Payment he wouldn't hear of, though I got him to consent to my supplying petrol for the bus. It was strange, though, how she always "happened" to be full when I arrived.

"Don't talk nonsense, Rory," was the only answer I got to the question of payment, "I'm going to get just as much fun out of having you and introducing you to the coast as I hope you are. Besides, I shan't hesitate to make use of you here if I need help—"

And with that I had to be content. In truth, I was; more than content. The empty game-book bogey looked as if he might be banished at last, and—next time I appeared it would be September.

3

SEPTEMBER 3

That year I watched September come in with more than usual trepidation, for Friday fell on the second, and William, in his last letter, had talked of partridges. But the clerk of the weather didn't let me down, and as I left London that night the sun was sinking behind me in a placid haze of red that augured well enough.

"I've got a walk for you tomorrow, anyway," William greeted me at the station. "If we can manoeuvre 'em right, there are several good coveys on the top land. Pheasants, too," he added meditatively. "My brother John's coming over tomorrow and he and Harry have had a standing feud on that point ever since John shot one in September two years ago. Now there's a fine of a couple of gallons of beer to Harry, who has been waiting to catch him ever since I" Lord, it was good to be down at the cottage again, and to realize that the whole arrangement hadn't been a dream. I sat down that evening to a supper of cold partridge which simply melted in my mouth. Half-accusingly, I looked at William—after all, it was only the second of the month! And William grinned.

"If I told you that bird was alive at lunch-time today, you'd maybe laugh. It's a fact, though; slain this afternoon specially for your benefit, and plucked and cooked while it was still warm. Sounds barbarous, I know, not hanging a bird. But if you don't give 'em time to stiffen before cooking—well, you're eating the result. You should know."

I was also learning; I never wish to eat a sweeter bird than that was.

When I got down to breakfast next morning, William had just come in from visiting the foxes. "Had to give Harry a hand with the chores, too," he said. "He'd hate to miss this first walk as much as I should! Looks like being a real scorcher of a day."

That hour after breakfast on the first shooting day of a new season—Belts filled, guns laid out, and Bill trembling with excitement, whining and thumping the floor with his tail, not daring for a moment to take his eyes off his master's face—

Then John arrived and, a moment later, Harry, complete with bag and stick, appeared at the window.

"Got any baby pheasants in your pocket today, Harry?" John greeted him.

"Ar, that we'll know come evening. Master John," was all the change he got, and we were off.

For me, the day that followed was purest gold. The weather was perfect—a few white woolly puffs of cloud in a sky of clearest blue, and a sun that was doing its rapid best to lick away the spangles of crystal which the morning mist had left on every leaf and cobweb. There were enough and more than enough partridges to keep us a-tiptoe every second, and the company was of the very best. What more could the heart of man desire on a September morning?

William's "top land" was a triangle of less than a hundred and fifty acres, with an alien boundary on two sides and his own fen below. The partridges, of course, evinced a decided preference for the alien boundaries; and our game, to keep them in play within the triangle, was none too easy, for the only cover was a square of sugar beet in the farthest corner and a big old pit of two or three acres in the middle that was full of shoulder-high bracken, broom and furze.

"Do we get any birds in there we'll ha' a job to find them," was Harry's comment.

There were two big stubbles on our way before we reached the roots.

"They won't be in there of their own accord," William said. "You'd think the partridges hereabouts would be educated to sugar beet by now, but they won't go near it unless they're pushed." He slipped on ahead along the boundary fence to act as a hint to any birds that the other direction might be safer, and we inclined out across the stubble behind him.

Oh, but it was good to feel the clean crisp crunch and thrust of stubble under foot once more, to catch a glimpse of tiny jewels of scarlet and bright blue, the eyes of pimpernel and speedwell creeping in among it that watched us passing; and the anticipation of the jump of the first covey!

Not that impatience was tried severely in that direction. They rose wild in front of John. Ten, twelve, fourteen of them I counted, well-grown birds and heading right, too. four pairs of eyes watched anxiously as they swung from gold to green, and I do not doubt four anxious prayers were offered up. Square in the middle of the roots the covey checked, fourteen spread tails for a second flickered red, and they were down.

Three other lots we saw, and two of them went right. The third skimmed on and on, and with a derisory flip just lifted the boundary fence safely ahead of William, hung set-winged for a second against the sky, then dropped beyond and so were out of court. Three coveys were in the roots, though, and we approached them full of hope. Harry was sent to mark the pit hole where we hoped to push them.

Backs to the boundary, across the drills we faced. And William waved us in. On and on and on—hesitant steps knowing each one would see them rise and catch me with my foot cross-balanced on a sugar beet. Then, with a whirl, two coveys rose together all around us and the air was a flurry of hurtling forms—seconds, too full to think—a feathered shape that crumpled, and another, glory be. Then a few grey feathers floating idly down to rest. Bill was busy, for we had five birds down between us, and most of the others had headed on for Harry, though a few swung right to safety—for today. From the third covey John got one, and William and I between us settled the hash of a pair of ancients that Bill put up all unexpectedly behind us. William was grinning from ear to ear as Bill brought in the last one.

"We'd have missed them altogether without him," he muttered. Harry had marked the other two lots down in the jungle—" And a master lot of French birds ran in when I came along," he added.

"One bird only at a time, and mark him like a plaster," were William's instructions. "This bracken doesn't give Bill a chance."

Back and forth we swung, and they rose in ones and twos till Harry's network bag began to bulge. It was heavy going, and Bill had twenty anxious minutes with a runner, while we could only mark his progress by the swaying bracken fronds. Very relieved I felt when he found it nearly a hundred yards away, for I had been responsible. A young cock pheasant clambered up from the bracken at my feet, his neck and breast still spattered with childhood's feathers. I glanced at Harry, but his face was firmly set, and he wouldn't meet my eye!

Many birds we left behind us, for the cover was almighty thick, and the day was hot. But quite a few we didn't, and by the time we'd finished it even Harry looked satisfied, and Bill was panting like a traction engine. And, miracle of miracles, not two hundred yards away there was the village pub! That beer was purest nectar.

"We'll give the fen a try this afternoon," William said, "and leave those top birds in peace. They've had quite enough of a roasting for a first time over. Though I doubt if we'll see much down there yet," he added as an after thought.

Of partridges we didn't see a lot. Two barren pairs to be exact; and three of these we slew. And once a covey—. On the fen edge, near the road, were several tiny fields with thick and straggling fences in between. We were taking two of these fields together, with John and I in one, and Harry and William beyond the hedge. I heard a covey rise, and William shoot. "Over, over," came a bellow from Harry. A flicker through a gap against the sky and I had shot—a pleasing snap, and I was almost sure my bird had crumpled. And in a minute, far too sure; for in the gap Harry appeared, trying to look bereaved, and holding up—a baby pheasant!

My plea of false pretences was disallowed, for two partridges had crossed the fence behind me and John got one of them. Be sure I paid my debt in full that evening, and for many days to come!

The rest of that covey had swung aside, and so we headed down on to the fen itself. It was a pleasant enough place for a walk even now when it was stony dry and the dykes were low, and I could well imagine what fun it could be in the winter when the snipe were there and pheasants were in season—one might meet anything. Two hares we saw, but they were sacred to the beagles; they fled with ears close pressed till they were out of danger, and then the black tips gaily rose and bobbed erect till they were out of sight. A single mallard clattered from a dyke quite close to where I'd spent my evening—could it be a whole fortnight ago?—and a snipe twisted from a bone-dry patch of rushes, but John was there and he didn't travel far.

"That's a great spot later in the year," William said when we foregathered, "though the snipe alone know why, as the fields on either side look exactly the same to me, and you never see a smell of one in them."

One cartridge only I fired that afternoon, and an expensive one at that. Yet never for an instant did time hang heavy. There was a mass to see, and all of it fascinating. A cock reed bunting, spotless in coal black hood and snowy collar, that flirted down a dyke, pausing to cling to a stem of meadowsweet and balancing there with a fan of his tail that showed twin streaks of white. A wing of plover that the sun struck black and silver. A kestrel, hovering in the speckless blue above. I wondered what he thought of all our doings from his vantage point up there; or the stock dove, flying so unconcernedly almost into shot before she saw us and flung aside with a speed and swerve that would have made a Messerschmidt look silly. Those, and a thousand other sights besides. I came to the conclusion that there was a lot more to a September day's shooting than just firing cartridges and killing stuff.

Soon after three o'clock we turned for home, and Harry set off at a tangent.

"There's one small bit I want to try before we call it a day," William said, "a broom patch hard by one of the most perfect spots for a drive you ever saw—if it wasn't on my boundary. I know there's one big covey we never met this morning that live thereabouts, and they might be in the broom for shade on an afternoon like this."

A perfect spot for a drive, William was right. A narrow gully, deeper than any railway cutting and not much wider, clove unexpectedly into the hill, and there we lined ourselves. On the bank ahead a flaming mass of foxgloves, past their best but still most lovely, caught the sun. They were set in a frame of bracken, and the skyline waved with the darker green of broom. Perfect indeed, not only for a drive.

"Look up, over." But we'd heard the whirr of wings, and Harry's yell was hardly necessary. Tense seconds, staring at that skyline, guns alert; and three birds fled over William who was on my right. Tiny, they looked, like starlings at that height. Frenchmen—I caught a glimpse of a barred flank in the sunlight, and two of the three fell clean, out of the sunlight and into the shadow where we were. And proudly Bill retrieved them.

"Sorry," said William, "but you can't tell where they'll go." Sorry! After that perfect right and left. I wouldn't have been.

A very ordinary day's partridge shooting—eleven brace and oddments. But I'd not have changed places with a king that day.

4

September 4

"I don't know what your ideas are on the subject of Sunday shooting," William remarked next morning at breakfast. "I'm afraid on the coast I do it pretty regularly when I can find the time, and it's a general practice. In fact, at times, the week-ends are a pretty fair menace down there!"

I was glad William had raised the point as I'd made up my mind to abide by his decision and to "do in Rome …". Nevertheless, I suspect it was largely on account of week-end visitors like myself that he did it, for he would never allow shooting inland on a Sunday. Nor did I ever know him to go down to the coast by himself on Sundays, whatever the weather. But I wasn't grumbling; my times were all too short in any case.

"Like to go down for a look-see, to-day? "he asked. "I can't manage to stay for the flight—which is hardly worth while in any case this time of year as most of the home-bred duck have collected together into biggish bunches. A lot have cleared off South altogether; and the foreigners haven't put in an appearance yet. We might take a walk along the sea wall, though."

I jumped at the idea, for I was longing to see my winter's campaigning grounds. Guns we collected, and Bill, and some bread and cheese for lunch. Presently the ancient motor roared into life, and we were off.

"The guns are more or less a token display," William remarked. "There's no point in ruining those shoes of yours, as we certainly would if we left the sea wall far. One thing you must invest in, and that's a pair of thigh boots. And it's worthwhile getting a decent pair while you're on the job. Rubber bars across the soles will save you a good deal of slipping about on the mud and wet grass, and a pair of them shouldn't cost you more than twenty-seven and six!"

"What's wrong with ordinary gum boots?" I asked. "They cost even less."

"Not worth the saving. It's not the depth of water you'll have to wade in so much as the fact that you'll be wanting to kneel a lot, and you won't have time to choose your spots.

"Clothes? Well, warmth, lightness, and invisibility are your three ideals. Especially warmth, you'll find, and everyone has his own infallible ideas on how to achieve them; but whatever you wear on top you'll get into the hell of a mess, don't forget. I'll only give you two small tips: a bit of fur round your jacket collar is more than comforting at times. Any old sort. I've simply stitched an old rabbit skin round mine, and it's far better value than any muffler. And for your feet, a dozen thicknesses of newspaper as in-soles for your thigh boots."

The car bumped off the road and headed up a lane whose surface grew progressively worse until it degenerated into a mere grass-grown track along which the old bus jumped and jolted till she came face to face with an enormous grass-grown dyke some thirty feet in height, and then perforce she stopped.

"Well, here we are," William announced. "That's the sea wall in front."

I don't quite know how in my ignorance I'd pictured a sea wall. Something big and strong and buttressed like the esplanade at a seaside resort, I suppose. Certainly not as a ridge which sloped at less than forty-five degrees, covered with bright green grass on which sheep were grazing! And then I noticed that beneath the grass were fitted blocks of stone and I realized how enormous its strength must be with that construction and that gentle slope. But the raging tides? No sign of sea whatever met my eyes when I climbed the ridge and got my first glimpse of what William referred to as "the coast".

At first sight the view was horribly unimpressive. At my feet the vivid green that covered the sea wall flattened out into a level width of finest turf that reached maybe ten or twenty yards out from its base. Then a coarser growth appeared, not grass at all, but duller flattened clumps, scattered at first, that gradually merged together into a sage-green mass that covered up the turf save in a few stray patches. Straight out for a quarter of a mile and as far as the eye could see to right and left this belt continued, till on its farther edge the grass took charge again; but a duller washed-out looking grass, half hidden by clumps of some straight-stalked plant that fringed right on to the naked mud. For beyond this strip of vegetation which made the saltings (a strip which varied all along the coast from over half a mile in width to a matter of yards) was mud, mud, mud. Close in, right up against the salting edge it shimmered vivid' green in patches, the green of a new-sown lawn when the first seeds start to shoot, but beyond it stretched for miles and miles, gleaming in varying shades of browns and greys and purples up to the horizon. A scattered line of posts with odd-shaped tops were the only things that broke that wild immensity, and they were tiny in the distance.

"Take a look through those," William handed me a pair of glasses. "Those black things are the tops of the buoys marking the channel. Water's dead low now, and the sea's seven or eight miles out, so the bulk of the buoys have dropped below the level of the mud banks. But you'll see quite big ships chuffing in and out on the tides."

Their tips most certainly were odd shapes; some round, some square, some built like cages, and five or six at least were cormorants! One old fellow was sitting on top of a cage with his wings hung limply out to dry and his beak stretched upwards like a beggar crying alms.

When we sat down for lunch, I noticed a few feet up from the base of the sea wall a line of debris that was unmistakably the leavings of the tide; odd bits of wood, the dried wing of a gull, a dog-fish's egg case—all resting on a basis of little oval leaves about an inch in length and quarter of an inch across. Idly I picked up a handful to examine.

"Crabgrass—sea-sage—obione," William forestalled my query. "That's the sagey looking stuff that covers most of these saltings. It hasn't got a flower to speak of, and the leaves float and carry the seeds about with 'em till the tide sows 'em. You'll find it useful to fill your bag with later to sit on; and in the winter it's about the only cover left on the saltings, as the sea asters—those tallish clumps growing out beyond it—simply wither into straight stalks that get flattened by the first ice-bearing tide.

"Yes, it's dry enough up here now. New moon was last Monday, so the tide responsible for that mark was probably on Monday night, or Tuesday morning. There's a later mark lower down."

There was too. More scattered and less distinct, for it was on the flatter surface barely clear of the obione clumps.

"How do I know when it was? Well, the moon's the lady who runs the tides. Roughly speaking, you'll find the peak, that is the spring tides, come just after the full and new moons, and in between whiles they slacken off to the neaps around the first and third quarters. So, provided you know what the moon's doing, you've a very fair idea the size the tide will be. And the time: different places vary, but each high water's about twenty-five minutes later than the one before it, and the hour after the full and new moon is always at the same time. That's roughly fifty minutes a day, so you can work it out from that.

"The peak tides themselves follow the same sort of routine too, and they get to their biggest on the new moons nearest the spring and autumn equinoxes. That'll be in about three weeks' time. Then's the time the sea walls and breakwaters all around the coast get a pretty fair testing, especially if there's anything like a wind to back the tide. I've seen the waters within six feet of the top of the wall where we're sitting now and tearing at it like demented things. That was on the September full moon the year the sea broke through near Hemsby, and it was a pretty impressive spectacle. The average spring at full and new moon barely gets to the foot of the wall, though, and the neaps don't always reach the saltings even."

William paused to light his pipe.

"That means I'm going to strike just about the same moons and tides each time I come," I hazarded.

"Correct; four or five days after the full and new moons. With any luck they won't be bad times either."

A low growl from Bill interrupted us. From a cottage quarter of a mile along the sea wall there appeared an old woman with a basket over her arm. Presently she struck out across the saltings.

"Samphire she'll be after," William said. "Poor man's asparagus; it grows all along the edge of the mud. Those bright green patches you can see. Round fleshy stalks about six inches high, rather like candelabra cacti without the spikes. You pick it roots and all, and when it's cooked hang on to the roots and pop the whole top in your mouth. The fleshy part strips off, and you're left with the hard core in your hand. Sort of vague salty taste of nothing in particular, not very exciting. A lot of the cottagers pickle it for the winter, and you get folk gathering it by the cart load to sell."

For the last few minutes I'd been watching several parties of large white birds gradually congregating over a dark patch in the mud. Even at that distance they didn't look quite like gulls. I took the glasses from William, and in place of a white mass, a clear-cut picture of black and white and chestnut and bronze came sprinting into my field of vision.

Shelducks, hundreds of shelducks, collected over an area where the mud was broken into a series of little black cliffs and valleys. A mussel bed, or scaup as William called it. It was a most intriguing picture, for the glasses were powerful enough to show me each bird in detail. Some were sifting in the mud as they walked along, their necks curved down and out in front of them, heads weaving from side to side like snow-pushers; others slept or basked in the sunshine, while on a tiny eminence a few feet from the rest three stood bolt upright, gravely nodding their glossy dark heads to one another for all the world like elders deciding the conduct of a school treat. They made a handsome trio as they stood there in the sun, no trace of the autumn moult showing in their showy black and white and chestnut livery. Even the coral of their beaks showed clear.

Nor were the shelducks the only occupiers of the mussel scaup. A couple of curlews stood pensively aloof, taking no notice whatever of their brilliant neighbours, and a score or so of dunlins ran mouselike in and out among the piled up shells. They were the busiest people of the lot, for their little legs were never still. As I watched, five more curlews arrived in a long low curve-winged glide, and pitched alongside the pair already there. One of these slowly raised his wings straight upwards. You could almost see him yawn and stretch on being waked. Then he took a couple of threatening steps towards the newcomers, decided they weren't worth worrying his head about after all, snuggled his long beak back in over his shoulder and settled down to sleep in the sun once more.

I lowered the glasses, and immediately the scene was just a white splash that well might have been gulls agleam in the sunlight on a patch where the mud showed darker.

I think a little of the magic of the place must suddenly have come flooding upon me, for almost without volition I turned to William, a-sprawl on the bank beside me.

"I'm going to like this coast of yours," I told him quite decidedly.

5

September 17

I must have thigh boots, William had said. Well, that was easy enough, in theory. But at what sort of shop does one get thigh boots in London? Boot shops? "Never heard of 'em"; at least, mine hadn't. Fishing tackle dealers? The ones I tried were more than anxious to fit me with complete sets of waders—stockings, boots and all —but thigh boots pure and simple, no. Eventually, I ran some to ground in a little shop down by the river that smelt of tar and ropes and leather, whose proprietor produced for my inspection thigh boots of such variety as I never knew existed. Red thigh boots, white thigh boots, black thigh boots, thigh boots with sloping tops and tops cut square; thigh boots with soles of leather or of wood; thigh boots with smooth soles or soles with rubber bars across them, succeeded one another till I was almost dizzy. White I ruled out. Red too. But the different types of soles tried me sorely. Finally, I chose a black pair with sloping tops and rubber bars to save me slipping on the mud. When these wear out my next pair will be the same.

When I got down to the cottage that week-end I found that Harry, alas, was ill, so William could not get away.

"But that's no reason why you shouldn't take the liver pill" (alias the ancient motor) "down to where we were last time and get a bit of the local geography into your head," he added. "High water will be about ten o'clock, so you won't have to worry about being cut off."

I felt almost like an explorer as I topped the sea wall next morning, complete with gun, and wearing my new thigh boots. What I should meet I'd very little notion, but whatever it was would be new; and maybe something would find its way into the larder.

The coast wore a very different garb from that of the other day of blazing sunshine. The sky was overcast with dull grey clouds scudding low before a wind from the south-east that was quite cold enough to discourage any lingering. And the sea—there really was a sea this time— a grey-brown monster that had converted all the mud into a level dun expanse of gently heaving waters and thrust out tentacles to cover nearly a third part of the saltings.

For a moment or two I stood on the bank and watched. With not a soul in sight it was almost daunting to set forth into that emptiness; although later I grew to value that same emptiness as a pearl beyond price and to feel almost aggrieved if there was another soul in sight. Today it was new to me, and strange, for the saltings looked entirely devoid of life.

Looked; and from the sea wall only. For with every step I took, it seemed, more life disappeared. Little trips of dunlins, invisible till they rose, fled with a shrill "scree-e" as I squelched along as close to the tide edge as I dared; redshanks screamed alarm as they twisted low away, to rise with an upward lift and swing around to see exactly who it was disturbed their solitude; and from a patch of open grass three curlews, majestic among the smaller fry, rose in a whirl of brown and white to send a clear "curlee" a-whistling down the saltings.

A horde of finches, linnets in the main, looped twittering into the air and circled round to vanish as they pitched again behind me.

The whole place was enchanted, the sea sage a magic carpet. Birds—fascinating birds, so very obvious when they flew, just vanished as they touched the earth again. And every step I took flushed more.

For over an hour I tramped, crossing and re-crossing creeklets whose bubbled surfaces were fast retiring sea ward. And for over an hour I got nothing but tantalizing flashes of white rumps, of silvered underwings a-whirl for a second as then- owner swung into the wind to turn and become just another dun shape scudding low away from me, nearly invisible against the mottled saltings.

Some times a whistle drifted back—the thin clear pipe of a lone grey plover, a whimbrel's three-pronged call, or the liquid music of a curlew, most beautiful of all. But the birds that made them were waiting not upon the order of their going, and never a one let me get close enough to dream of shooting. I should be going home with clean barrels unless I used a little thought, so I sat down on a creek edge to consider.

Surprisingly enough, it was warmer near the ground. The vegetation broke the wind a little, and reminded me that it was still September. The creek at my feet was three-parts empty, only a muddy flow that broke in tiny rapids and waterfalls as it met obstructions to its outward progress. My boots made fascinating things to play with as they dangled, and the waters ridged merrily around them. About me came mysterious gurgles and suckings as the crab-holes in the overhanging banks emptied them selves.

The saltings were now quite clear, and the mud was clearing rapidly. And as it cleared so was it peopled. It was amazing the way the saltings gave up birds. Hosts of dunlin that followed up the lip of each retreating wave; knots, in small parties, larger editions of the dunlin; here and there a redshank mincing on stilt-like legs well into the water. Grey plover, many still wearing their black chests of the summer months, came later, when the tide was lower. Curlew too—perhaps they thought it beneath their dignity to dodge the waves, for they seldom drew too near the water's edge; but as soon as a bank was fairly clear of water, hey presto! There they were.

I was so engrossed watching the steadily growing company that I completely failed to notice a whimbrel, which slipped upon me from my landward side. Be sure he noticed me! Even so, he was well within range, and I could clearly see his head and that long curved Jew boy's beak of his twist sideways to look at me as he flung away. But his luck was in, for he swung off to my right, and seated in the creek I couldn't bring my gun to bear in time.

Hell! This was no way to fill the pot. One elementary thing I had learnt, though. It was no use my walking after these wild birds. I must make them come to me or we should stay as strangers. On the ground, they were more or less invulnerable, therefore I must learn what made them fly, and when, and where.

Tides obviously, and food. As they could not feed under water, or ride the tides, they must move ahead of them when the waters came to cover the mud. And equally, they would hurry back as soon as the mud was bare again, for then the feeding would be richest. Around high water seemed my time, for then they would perforce be on the saltings, which afforded me at least a little cover.

Curlee! Curlee! The high call jerked me round to face the land. A little bunch of half-a-dozen curlew were sliding out—straight at me. No, not quite. Within a hundred yards they passed, quite low, and flattened and pitched out on the mud. A minute after another lot appeared, and after them a single bird. They passed me, too, a hundred yards away. Was that their flight line? I left my creek and hurried over to be beneath the next lot, and the next lot came just over where I'd left. And the lot following that. If only I'd stayed put! Should I move back? I wavered; and then realized that I'd been a fool to move at all, for they were coming out both sides of me, so that I must be in their line. And I was hidden; so why move at all?

Firmly, I stayed. But alas, the little flight was over, and no more curlew came. But, what had they been doing in land anyway? Had the tide moved them, and they, not content with the pickings on the saltings, flown in to try their luck among the fields, and been warned by some mysterious inner alarm clock the moment the mud banks were uncovered?

Later I learnt that something of the sort was true. For the curlew, perhaps more than any other of the wading tribes, crosses the sea bank indiscriminately as the spirit and his tummy move him. He is truly cosmopolitan in his search for food, and almost every tide provides a flight of sorts.

But today I'd missed the boat. For a long time nothing moved along the saltings edge where I was sitting, so presently I decided to explore a little.

These saltings, which had seemed a perfect maze of endless aimless creeks, proved rather interesting, for I found the creeks were anything but aimless. Each was part of a perfect natural drainage system calculated to dry its catchment area as quickly as possible. Thousands of tiny runnels took the surface water from near the sea wall, and joined and joined again till they had achieved channels several feet across and three or four feet deep. These bigger creeks, after much meandering to pick up further tributaries, gradually joined forces, till by the time they reached the mud there was one channel only, by which the surface waters of probably a mile of saltings wove their way across the flats and to the sea. So when the tide flowed the waters rose first up this channel, up the branching creeks, and up the myriad tiny runnels till finally, if the tide was big enough, they overflowed, and the whole saltings were awash. And when it turned they emptied back the way they came, by a drainage system proven twice a day for centuries.

One thing I noticed. Where the obione grew thickest and so held back the tide the most, the creeks were many more, and deeper than on the grassy patches, and with the heavy overhanging clumps they gave most perfect cover. Indeed, in the case of some of the smaller runnels, the cover grew right over them and they made most perfect traps for the feet of the unwary. Clear of the binding vegetation of the saltings the channels flattened out and grew much wider, till the soft mud cliffs that held them in were seldom more than eighteen inches high, and in most parts lower still. That was a messy place to try and hide in, as I discovered. For as I was following a channel out I saw a long low line of birds skimming the flats towards me. Black they looked, head on—big, too, and flying evenly spaced out. Curlew? Or even duck? No time to look more closely. A little cliff of mud offered some cover, and towards that I floundered. Its base was sticky, very sticky, and I felt my knees sink softly in. So did the hand I threw out to try to keep my balance. But I found the cover was better than I'd dared to hope, for the banks above the "cliff" loomed imperceptibly up so that my sky hue was a matter of feet only. Frantically I glanced from side to side along it. Then—for a second—wings! Swoosh! and eighteen panic-stricken shelduck fanned vertically against the leaden sky. They made a wonderful picture as they hung there; each feather showed distinct. But I was out for blood; straight overhead a vivid shape in black and white and chestnut was wildly climbing—and at the peak of his climb he crumpled, whirling down over and over, thump into the mud beside me.

Gloatingly I smoothed his feathers.... My first shot on the saltings....

William, that evening did much to puncture my complacency. For a long time he stared at my trophy without speaking. Then:

"I always think the words of an old keeper at home ought to be made to apply particularly to the saltings. I'd shot a buzzard one day, and the old man was justly peeved. 'What you shoots you'd ought to be made to eat. Master William' he told me, 'then maybe you'd be a mite more particular with your cartridges'."

My gun caused me grief that night, too. Even in that short space of time the salty mud had eaten through the blueing on the barrels, and it fitted together and opened grittily. I went to bed in rather a pensive mood....

6

October 1

William, I was forced to admit, had proved right. A second gun of some sort was necessary if I was going to do the coastal shooting I hoped to. Despite having spent upwards of an hour on it as soon as I'd got back, my beloved Churchill had not been improved by its day on the coast. Even now I could see the marks where my muddy fingers had gripped the blueing on the barrels, and that crunch when first I had opened and closed the breech had been pure agony. William had advised it, and even the train that rattled me back to London in the grey of the Monday morning had muttered all the way—"You must get a gun—you must get a gun."

That was a fortnight ago; and I had succumbed to the temptation. In the rack above my head as I travelled back once more was my new gun. At least, it wasn't quite my gun yet, as in spite of my first impulse, I'd only got it on approval. But I was very anxious to hear William's verdict on it, as it was the result of much searching and appeared to be about the only gun in London that fitted both my requirements and my purse. It had been built specially for wildfowling, was heavily choked both barrels, chambered for three-and-a-quarter-inch cartridges, an ejector, weighed eight and three-quarter pounds, and as a special feature the rib had been cross-hatched with a file to help it show up in bad light or by the moon. It was a nice-looking weapon, black and polished specklessly.

When I reached William's station a slight contretemps arose, for it was inky dark and I'd no light for my velocipede. But the station-master proved more than equal to the difficulty, for he produced an enormous porter's lamp, which he proceeded to lash to my handlebars with a length of rope, and so caparisoned I pedalled off towards the cottage.

William was waiting for me, and so was supper, and supper just beat impatience. But the very moment I'd swallowed the last mouthful I undid the case and produced my new toy for inspection.

Rather to my disappointment, William was strictly non-committal. He examined it minutely, hefted it, balanced it, and ran his finger slowly down the roughened rib with out a word. Then:

"You've got it on approval? Good. With any luck you'll get a fair chance of trying it out tomorrow, as I thought we might go and lie up on the tide in the morning. It's high about ten o'clock which is a nice easy hour as we can breakfast here and be down there by eight-thirty. The saltings are always rather fun this time of the year in the day-time, as the big wader migrations are in full swing, and you never quite know what you're going to meet next…"

The place we fetched up at next morning was new to me. William drove the car into a farmyard, where an old man carting straw waved cheerfully to him and assured us it would be all right. Followed by Bill we started out beside a narrow dyke which separated a field of late potatoes from a stubble where a tractor plough was slicing over clean furrows of jet black earth—to the evident delight of a wavering mob of black-headed gulls whose screaming bid fair to drown the pantings of its engines. Half a mile ahead rose the green bank of the sea wall; between us and it and on all sides clear to the unrelieved horizon the land stretched flat as a pancake, cut into squares and rectangles of black or green or yellow by dykes as straight as rulers.

It was a dour land, hard with the burden of its riches—as if the deep black soil was rated too valuable to squander in mere adornment. Every inch was under cultivation, and efficiency was the keynote everywhere. Dykes which served to drain the land took the place of hedges. Vast greenhouses served to hasten on the plough by housing the seed potatoes for next year's crop. The only trees that curbed the flat monotony were wind-breaks planted round the dwellings, and even the houses themselves lacked graciousness. Square and sturdy, they served their purpose and were sufficient to it.

A young land won and held from the sea by force, yielding its treasures a hundred-fold to those strong enough to hold it and labour hard by it, but lacking the mellowness the centuries had bestowed upon its older neighbours. Even now, lapped in the placid sunshine of early autumn, it looked a land of little ease. But by its very singleness of purpose it held a certain grim attraction peculiarly its own.

Within a hundred yards of the sea wall Bill, who had been following quietly at William's heel, made a sudden dive down into the dyke, and with a terrific crackle and bustle and flurry a cock pheasant burst up and out almost into our faces. I could have smacked him down with my gun barrels, so close he passed. An angry orange eye glared for a second into mine, a flash of greeny purple iridescence above a snowy ruff; black tippets on deep bronze that paled to ruddy gold; and the vision passed, long tail a-quiver as he sailed away from us.

October the first! As pretty a little reminder as one could wish for.

"All the same," William remarked, "I often wish there weren't any of the brutes down here at all. Occasionally, very occasionally you meet one outside the sea wall. Partridges too, sometimes, and hares; which is all very nice, as I reckon they're fair game there. Trouble comes when some b.f. sees game inland—and gives chase. Naturally enough the farmers try to stop it, and their simplest method is to close all private ways down, which accounts for ninety per cent of 'em. Can't blame the farmers. I'd do it myself like a shot. But it's the devil of a nuisance all the same. To get where we're going today would mean a seven-mile tramp if we hadn't been able to cut across these fields!"

Abruptly the dyke we'd been following debouched into what was almost a small river moving sluggishly along the base of the sea wall and spanned by a single greasy looking plank. To our right the river spread into an open pan some thirty feet across, mud collared like a salting pool, that pear-shaped in towards a brick culvert in the wall itself down which the water gurgled. On the mud rim of the pan two dunlins were busy probing, and over-shadowing them, the larger daintier figure of a redshank bobbed jerkily to its reflection. Only a glimpse of him we got; then in a flirt of black and white with orange legs a-trail he was away over the bank, and his mocking whistle came ringing back to us and warning all the saltings that something of danger was afoot.

Beyond the wall the stream emerged from the culvert by a pair of sluice gates. A full-blown creek already, which carved a winding channel for itself towards the distant mud.

"One each side, and when you get to the salting edge find yourself a hideyhole fifty-sixty yards out from the main creek. I'm going to put Bill in the middle."

Those were William's instructions. The last remark was a little above my head, but following his example I stuffed my canvas game bag with handfuls of the dry wiry old grass that grew along the base of the bank, and after a quarter of an hour's hectic stumbling through crabgrass and into and over runnels, found myself a hideyhole as he had said. A little beauty it was, too; a nice three-foot-deep creek in whose bank I kicked an armchair seat, lined it with my bag and settled down.

Then I looked round for William. His actions, to say the least of it, struck me as rather queer. For on the very bank of the main creek, in the middle of the most obvious clump of crabgrass available, he built up a nice dry seat and proceeded to park Bill firmly on top of it before he hid himself some fifty yards beyond.

Bill, sitting on his pyramid and looking supremely self-conscious in his isolation, was obvious as day to anything flying low up the main creek. Then I began to appreciate William's strategy, for anything coming up the creek seeing Bill there would probably feel nervous, swing aside—and William and I were there to welcome them.

But presently I found there was a good deal more to it than that. A curlew, passing well behind us over the saltings on business of his own, saw something peculiar sitting on a clump of crabgrass, and straightaway glided over to investigate. It was an unwise move on his part, for he passed quite close to William, so profited little from his curiosity.

Bill evidently did not think much of curlews. His face, when he returned to his eyrie after taking William the corpse, was a study. Lips wrinkled, licking a last feather distastefully away—just like a child who has bitten into a red-cheeked apple and found it a crab. But he returned to his seat at a wave from his master's hand. Mentally I doffed my hat to William's training.

That hour produced some fascinating shooting. Redshanks came following the creeks in ones and twos, as often as not invisible below its banks until they saw Bill and veered screaming—generally to give one or other of us a chance. Horribly difficult to hit I found them, too. Once a greenshank appeared, larger and straighter flying than his cousin, with longer trailing leg. Mercifully he swung to William who spared him, for I doubt if I'd have spotted him in time. Dunlins, nice friendly little chaps, flew gaily up the channel ignoring Bill entirely, as if they knew they were too small to be in danger. Curlew gave us a deal of fun, but whereas the shank followed the creek and flared outward to bypass Bill, they for the most part kept well wide of it until they saw him, then curiously swung in to look more closely.

One thing only there was to mar my complete enjoyment. Whether my gun was too heavy to swing quickly or whether it was just the cramped position, I found my shooting growing worse and worse. A curlew came gliding in set-winged at Bill, to whirl with a deep throaty call straight at me. A gift from Heaven, and I sped him on his way. Another, slightly wider, and the same thing happened. Three shank in a row, and I missed them all; and when finally I did get a curlew, although he was a fair way out, both legs and wings were broken, and he was very dead indeed. I didn't like to blame the gun entirely for my rotten shooting, but I must confess I rather wondered, and my confidence was sadly shaken.

By now the sea was visible, a level line away out on the mud that here and there creamed gaily white as the sun picked up the foam crest of a flattening wavelet. Presently the outward flowing trickle of the creek I sat in was crushed back by a muddy bore that licked in hungrily. Once there, it was amazing how swiftly the bubble-flecked water rose; within ten minutes I was crouching on the bank.

They were exciting minutes, though, for the tide-edge-running waders were closing in on us. Godwits, grey plover, knots—I could see them all, lifting in little bunches and dropping back again a few yards farther on before the waves. But never farther than they need. It was developing into a race against time—whether they'd be forced within range of my hiding place before the tide forced me to leave it.

The result, I think, was a fair dead heat. I was half kneeling, half crouching on my elbows. Three godwits circled in over the rapidly shrinking strip of mud in front, and as I straightened for the shot my feet found the bottom of the creek; but whereas my waders were twenty-eight inches in length, the water must have reached quite thirty. However, I picked my first godwit and later on I ate him with delight.

A strenuous half-hour ensued, following back before the tide as it encroached upon the saltings; crouching in a patch of crabgrass till it was awash and a beastly chilly feeling around the knees told that the sea had once more triumphed over thigh boots and a rush to another clump a few yards closer inshore was imperative. William had sent Bill back clear of the tide, for his period of usefulness was over; but even so it was surprising that any birds came near us; for what we were appeared most obvious. Nevertheless we both got quite a bit of shooting. Knots, grey plover, even a whimbrel, all gave us chances as they passed up or down the tide line. Collecting them from the sea was tricky, though, for the muddy surface covered a multitude of creeklets and you never knew whether your next step would land in six inches or four feet of water. On the whole I was glad I'd got my boots full early—it saved such a lot of worry.

After a while the birds stopped moving and imperceptibly the waters started dropping back. William hailed me from across the creek— "We've had the cream of it. How about home and a dry change?"

I didn't take much persuading. Oh, but my boots felt heavy as I dragged them towards the sea wall, and the water flopped about inside. Yet when I took them off so little emptied out, and the air struck icy cold on my dripping feet.

From the top of the bank I looked back to where we'd been. Already a strip of mud was showing, and the sun picked flecks of white from among the lines of little waves that washed it.

Inland a curlew called. Soon they would be flighting out again to see what the tides had left them. But…

"Four is as many as we can cope with, along with the other stuff we've got," William said gently.

It was an interesting collection that we laid out in the back of the car. Besides the curlew, there was a whimbrel which might have been a dwarf among them save for the two broad stripes running back over his crown, making it look like dark hair neatly parted in the middle and brushed straight back. Grey plover we had, one with the rusty remains still of his black summer vest—extraordinarily like a golden, save for that dusky splash beneath his wings and the rudimentary hind toe; the same wide head and lovely liquid eye, same build, same size almost, and plumage marked the same and very near as bright. Small wonder people made mistakes so easily. Four redshanks, studies in black and white and soft grey brown above, with legs a brilliant splash of colour. Some knots, fat dumpy little fellows, bigger than a snipe—and my godwit, with his long and slightly upturned bill.

"Reckon we'll keep him and the knots ourselves," William said. "You'll find they'll take a bit of beating on the table."

My gun rather shook me when I came to clean it, for I had got it even muddier than the time before. The salt splashes on the barrel were already biting into the black, and the rib, with its rough cut surface, was an ugly sight. I'd been pondering my morning's performance with it rather seriously, and presently I asked William point-blank for his advice.

He lit his pipe, and considered for some time before replying.

"Well, for what it's worth," he said at last, "in my opinion you've got hold of the wrong weapon for an all-round job. It's too cumbersome, and far too heavily choked. You hear a lot talked about wildfowling consisting of shots at extreme ranges and the super choke has become rather a fetish. Maybe if you're going to confine your attentions purely to morning and evening flights at geese, it has its place; but there is a lot more to coast shooting than just that. Days like today, for instance, and more especially widgeons flighting under the moon. However thrilling it is to pull a bird out of the clouds occasionally you do quite often get close shots, and they're the ones that fill your bag. A mangled bird's no pride or pleasure to anyone. For all-round purposes I'd get a gun not more than quarter choke right and full, but not too full, left. Different makers vary in their ideas of full choke. After all, with three-inch shells that should give you a certain killing range up to sixty yards. And sixty yards in fact is a damn sight farther than you'd imagine, to hear some folk talking of their shooting exploits.

"That high file cut rib is an abomination. Useless in practice, and the very devil to clean. Ejectors are a moot point for coastal work. Nice, but unnecessary and so much extra mechanism to go wrong. What you want to aim at is as strong and simple an action as possible, and a plain gun, a shade shorter and straighter in the stock to allow for extra clothes, that'll take all the caning you're bound to give it and come back for more.

"It's a bad time of year to be looking for a second-hand gun just now. The end of the season is always better than the beginning, but I've marked one or two adverts in that Shooting Times that might appeal to you. That is, if you decide not to hang on to your present weapon."

I looked. Lists and lists of guns, and lists and lists of prices. Some within my reach. One in particular I liked the sound of:

12 b 3″ hammerless non-ejector 28″ barrels. R. imp. cyl., L. full choke. Good working order—any reasonable trial. Box X. £12.

That "any reasonable trial" had an honest ring about it, so on the strength of there being no time like the present I sat down straight away and wrote asking for it to be sent to me at William's address, "on a week's trial."

After all, I assured myself in bed that night, I hadn't really committed myself to anything. But I was glad I hadn't followed my original impulse and bought that other gun outright.

7

OCTOBER 2

It was boiling hot and muggy the next day. William and I spent the morning chopping up logs, and as Harry said when he passed, we both of us "wholly sweat". William looked up and caught my eye.

"Reckon it'd be cooler down along the sea wall?" he asked, and I gave the only answer possible to an honest nature. So as soon as we'd prepared the foxes' evening meal we left it for Harry to deliver, and sallied forth.

"Hardly worth while lugging that blunderbuss of yours down," William had said. "This time o' year a duck's the biggest thing that's likely to surprise you, and if any plover come out you'll need to be pretty nippy. Besides, we shan't get muddy."

So, rather dubiously, I had brought my Churchill.

We had a longish trek along the top of the sea wall to reach the hunting grounds which William had in mind, and well before we got there I'd decided that thigh boots were never meant to walk in in that weather. He, I noticed, wore an ancient pair of shoes, so ancient that they let the water out as well as in!

Odd redshank cursed us as we passed, and one old curlew

feeding close into the sea wall swore hoarsely as he took himself away.

"Pity we didn't spot him first," William muttered.

In an angle where the sea wall elbowed sharply inland, the saltings were covered with long dry grass, knee-high and tangled. William struck out across, and waved me up alongside to make a beat of it.

"I've met odd things that didn't quite belong here before now," he said with a twinkle, "and it's on our way."

It wasn't a lordly pheasant that we met though, but a small blue hawk that dashed out of a clump of grass almost at my feet, with a furious chik-chik-chik. Low over the grass tops he sped like a little blue bullet, then swung and soared back round us, a perfect falcon shape in miniature. It was a cock merlin, and behind the tuft I found the reason for his rage; a meadow pipit, freshly killed. It seemed strange to meet him here, so far away from the moors and heather of his home.

Presently the salting belt grew narrower, as the mud bit into it in a wide curved bay that reached within a few yards of the bank.

"Here's where I want to wait," William said. "There's grassland inside the sea wall and sometimes quite a few plover flight out from it on to the mud at night."

I was quite ready to stop, for my boots were fast becoming an affliction, and presently two pipes were glowing peacefully on top of the sea wall. It was barely five o'clock, so we'd over an hour to wait for darkness.

Behind us lay a close-fed pasture; a vivid emerald splash which reached right back to a second wall just like the one we lay on. Evidently the land between was fairly recently reclaimed, for the scars where the former salting creeks had run were still quite visible. Cattle, sleek and well-liking, grazed peacefully with half-a-dozen sturdy-looking shires standing a little way apart; and dotted all over the field were plover. There must have been several hundred there, most of them sleeping off their latest meal in the quiet sunshine; though one or two restless spirits still kept hunting, running a few quick steps and tipping forward like mechanical toys to offer a glimpse of dainty buff-and-white undergarments as they bent to gather some choice morsel.

One fellow, coveting a titbit discovered by his neighbour, rushed at him open-winged—a picture in black and silver that would have graced a Japanese screen. The neighbour did not wait to argue with him, but quietly slipped aside.

That neighbour though—somehow he did not look quite like the others. Then gradually I spotted several not quite like——; fully a quarter of the birds before us there were goldens! It struck me how very odd it was that two such vastly different coloured birds as green and golden plover could on the ground appear so very similar. Even when we'd quite established that both sorts were there it wasn't easy to distinguish which was which. Almost it seemed each bird reflected something of the colour of their common background.

The golden put rather a different complexion on affairs. With the best will in the world I'd not been able to work up much enthusiasm over the prospect of shooting those floppy old greens. But golden ... they fell into a different category altogether.

Slowly the sun was slipping lower, and gradually the sky began to put on such a colour as I have seldom seen; a rose-red flush which climbed clear overhead and deepened into glowing crimson that almost seemed to throb in its intensity. It truly looked as if the sun went down into a bath of blood beneath two lowering banks of soot-black cloud that frowned upon its passing. As I watched spellbound, across that crimson glory came shimmering a dancing column as of gnats on a summer's day; only these were martins, hundreds and hundreds of martins swirling in a dizzy saraband up and up till the topmost dwindled and were lost to sight. Slowly the column wound clear over me, still climbing, and passed diagonally across the saltings into the darkling eastern sky.

It was a wonderful sight, and in a setting worthy of any wonders. Nature had staged a most impressive send-off for them on their migrant journey, and I wondered how these shores would look to them on their return.

On the grasslands beside us the plover were becoming restless. Now and again one called, a long-drawn plaintive note, and once a golden piped.

William bestirred himself.

"We'd best be getting down on to the saltings," he said. "Only a few yards out so that we have anything coming low over the bank in silhouette 'stead of the boot being on the other foot."

Three hundred yards apart we settled, so as not to have to worry over safety angles if birds flew in between us. As I got down into a creek five birds tipped low over the bank to my left. Big redshank size they looked, and very like in build; only their wings were straighter, and they seemed to fly on a far more even keel. Just for a moment I held that clear-cut glimpse before they dipped and the loom of the sea wall hid them. Likely they were just shank, I thought, for I couldn't place them otherwise; but at the back of my mind I wasn't wholly satisfied.

A shrill whistle from William made me look round hastily. Coming in off the sea was a low black line, knotting and stringing out again as it drew nearer. Duck, and a goodly bunch of them! Low over the mud they came, then started lifting as they reached the salting edge. Why hadn't I brought the blunderbuss after all? Lower and lower I cowered in my creek. One end of the line should nearly pass above me—I could hear them gabbling and their hurrying wing-beats—after all, they weren't so very high. But as luck ruled it even the magnum wouldn't have helped me. Ever so slightly they altered course and the nearest passed a hundred yards away. By the time they reached the wall the line had split up into three V's, notching into one another. And so they dwindled into specks and pin-point lines which vanished across the fading redness of the sunset.

Minute by minute that redness dropped away and in its place a ghostly sliver of a moon grew swiftly clearer. From the east the light was gone, and the deep blue sky held little promise of a background.

Then with a rush the plover started coming. Black shapes for a second limned against the sky low over the seabank, then whirling, swerving, tumbling—vanishing as they dived below its level to skim the saltings and re appear head-high and corkscrew wildly upwards—pause, and fling away. A cry, sometimes a deep-toned "frow, frow, frow," of wings—and the night had swallowed them. Floppy old greens—these whirling dervishes? In the next few minutes my shell-belt grew much lighter without the bag increasing correspondingly.

My eyes glued on the top of the sea wall. Take them up there I must, or never. A dozen, swift-winged shapes, straight flying, coming at me clear against the sky—and I dropped a perfect right and left.

I found them both, moreover; but they weren't the goldens I'd expected. Long-legged, with a redshank's beak, their colour looked plain brown with odd spaced darker flecks above, and pale beneath. One was two inches longer than the other. I slipped them in my pocket. No time to worry now.

But the plover flight was over, and all too soon only the very west held any gleam of light.

Then a low whistle, and another. A swelling arpeggio of sweet clear pipes, and with a thrilling rush straight over me a wing of golden plover swept out and were gone. Perhaps a star face blinked a second as they came between, but the deep blue sky held back the secret of their passing, and they went their way unheedful of the danger they had left.

I heard a thump as William leapt a creek, and presently Bill, questing on ahead, brushed up against me. His master's figure loomed up in the darkness, and together we made our way back to the car.

As the headlights clicked on I produced my pair of bodies.

"Whew! You miserable sinner," William exclaimed. "They're ruffs. Or rather ruff and reeve!"

It was bad luck, but I'll swear the angel Gabriel himself couldn't have told them in that light.

Ruffs, merlin, that amazing flight of martins, all in one crowded hour; and the glory of that sunset has not faded yet.

8

October 15

Blue skies, hot sun, and calm quiet sunsets had sped the fortnight past, and once more I was down at the cottage with a large supper in front of me, and an excitingly solid-looking package lying across the arms of a chair alongside waiting to be opened. And once more supper missed the attention it deserved.

Strong sacking, a wooden framework, and rolls and rolls of corrugated paper. The parcel had surely been well packed. Better indeed, than the weapon which emerged from the multifarious wrappings at first sight seemed to warrant. For the stock was scratched and battered till all sign of polish or varnish had left it. The metal work of the lock and breech and trigger guard was brown with a fine and well-oiled rust, and the barrels—well, the barrels were encased in paint, grey paint, and rather chipped at that. But the face of the breech was free from any sign of pitting around the pin-holes and the inside of the barrels, after we had pushed a load of Vaseline from out of them shone bright as a mirror. Moreover, the gun assembled fitted tight with no sign of shake or rattle.

"She's had hard work all right," said William judicially, "but she's been well-cared for from the look of things, and seems sound enough. I don't awfully like those painted barrels, though. Rust's apt to eat away underneath the paint, especially along the rib, and before you know it you've a burst barrel on your hands. If you think of getting her I'd strip the paint and have a darn good look first. She seems honest enough otherwise, though."

That one word summed her up exactly. No frills, no flashiness, but a plain and honest hack. And as she looked, she was. The advertisement was true in every detail.

"Early rise tomorrow, my lad," William said when we'd done discussing the weapon in front of us. "Yesterday I was down at a spot—west of where you've been yet— where I'd heard a rumour of geese." Geese! I pricked up my ears. "Nary sign though. Only a few mallard that came out very early on. It was only just after full moon, so the geese may have stopped inland all the time, though I doubt it for I hung on till past midday. But I did see a master lot of curlew collecting on a mussel scaup as the tide came in. It'll be a case of digging in, which means an early start in any case with a ten o'clock tide, so we might as well go the whole hog and try a morning flight as well. Don't expect much, though." He added, as an after thought, "The moon won't be down till after dawn, which generally means a ragged flight with most of the stuff coming out before it's light enough to see."

All the same, it was with a high heart I set about getting things ready. Gun, boots and clothes laid out, cartridge belt filled. That was exciting, for William handed me four 3-inch BBs.

"Just in case," he said, "I always fill the pouches just to the left of my belt buckle with BBs, so that I know just where to grab if I am caught short."

I noticed another thing about William's belt. At one end of the cartridge pockets hung an extractor, and at the other a beautifully compact little compass, attached to the leather by small split rings. He saw me looking at the compass.

"You see, I got lost in a fog out on the mud once." He murmured, "Grab a handful of those long fours for the light. I reckon short stuff's good enough for most daytime messing about this time of year. Or widgeon, if they're reasonably close as they generally are under the moon. And if you have them dipped in lacquer like those," nodding towards a wooden box half-filled with shiny-looking ordinary Eley-Kynoch orange-coloured cases, "you don't lose many through swelling. Saves eight bob a hundred over the long 'uns too, which is a very definite consideration!"

It was a tip that saved me many shells that winter. For convenience sake I got William to get my cartridges where he ordered his, and the lacquering only cost me sixpence more a hundred. The whole of the paper part was dipped so that it was sealed in a sheath completely waterproof. These particular shells William had had loaded with modified smokeless Diamond and 1⅛ ounces of No. 6 shot, for he claims that of all the slow-burning powders, one of which such a load entails, modified S.D. gives the least flash at night. Far be it from me to lay the law down over various loads, but for its work I found that combination singularly effective.

It was pitch dark when I woke next morning with William bending over me. For a second I wondered, then memory flooded back. Clothes, boots, shells, gun; and a cup of sergeant-major's tea to set us off. Bill begged to come as well, but William firmly sent him back.

"We'll be out on the mud where a dog's more trouble than he's worth, and he'd only get unnecessarily cold and wet."

Outside it was lighter than I'd expected, for a near full moon was perched on top of a heavy bank of cloud that hid the west horizon, and the rest of the sky was clear and starry. What breeze there was came gently from the west, and even at that hour held little bite. It might have been spring, not autumn.

Half an hour later, when the car jerked to a standstill, I stepped out into soft dry sand, and when I stooped a spear of marram pricked my wrist. This was a very different land. William thrust a folded groundsheet at me, and I could see he held another and a sturdy little shovel in his hand.

"We'll not dig in till light," he said, "better follow me till we're clear of the dunes. There's a biggish channel outside where we'll lie up for the flight."

Then the headlights clicked off, and the night closed darkly in on us for the moon was now behind the cloud bank which had crept up over half the sky. Soft padding, ghostly quiet, through dry and shifting sand; the only sound the scrabble of a blade of marram or sea-holly sprig against our rubber boots and the frow of corduroy. In and out of dunes we moved till I began to wonder if William really knew the way; but suddenly we sloped sharply downwards, a pebble clinked, and we crossed a narrow belt of shingle. Firm going at last! Then splash!—and squelch, squelch, squelch; we were on level mud. No saltings here it seemed, for William headed straight out over it.

Lord, but I was warm. Those slippery dunes had been hard work, and the mud was of the type that grips like glue for the top half-inch. Ahead of us a jagged chasm yawned, with narrow coal-black clefts debouching from its sides; a chasm which resolved itself as we approached into a twenty-foot-wide channel with mud cliffs five feet high, the clefts just emptied creeklets, cut by those lazy waters that had missed the outgoing tide in their hurry to rejoin it. The channel floor was hard, and the waters at present in it shallow.

William moved on and left me in the perfect cover afforded by the elbow of a creeklet from which I could gaze towards both land and sea. Landwards for the duck I hoped would soon come out, and seawards—well, curlew I told myself; but William's rumour would not be altogether stilled. Geese—why shouldn't I dream of geese?

Those minutes of darkness after you're in place, before the morning flight is due to start, bring some the keenest joys of fowling. Only the sea and the wind and the flats for company in your little world, a world which grows quickly as the darkness lifts to show you—what? During the next half-hour. Fortune may send the answer to the dreamings of a lifetime. Wise woman, she never does completely, or future flights would lose much of their savour.

Ss-ss-ss-ss-ss-ss-ss. Blazes, but it was pitchy dark. They sounded low enough. Mallard from off the land—I heard them chuckle softly as they passed.

Again I heard wings, and once again. Surely it must grow lighter soon?

I strained my eyes; grey drifting into blackness with a solid bar of black upon the mud a hundred yards away that might have been a tree-trunk—or an alligator! I'd not seen that before; my world was growing, even though those duck were still outside it.

Minutes, tense minutes passed. This time I heard the deep-toned cack-ack-ack—quiet talk of stubbles rich in gleanings discovered in the night—before the music of their wing beats reached me. A black V speeding seaward high above. Too high, my reason told me.

But the grey gun knew better. Almost without consulting me she spoke; and the black V broke in fragments climbing wildly— all but one. And that one's outline blurred, grew larger and larger at an agonizing speed, and thwack! My mallard hit the mud with a bump that fairly raced my pulses.

One pellet, in the neck; and later I discovered that the left-hand pouch against my belt buckle was empty!

There is no moral. I never should have fired, for I despise an "optimistic" shot. Nevertheless, I think it was that fluky pellet that clinched the fortunes of the old grey gun for the next few years; and I only hope she has enjoyed her share of the pleasure she has given me.

That mallard when I picked him was not a pretty sight. The patch of mud he'd hit was soft above and black beneath and so was he, for the force of his falling had rinsed it through his feathers to the skin.

No doubt about the daylight coming now. My alligator was nothing but a bend in the channel where the far cliff loomed up black. I settled back to wait. That single shot began and ended my participation in the flight. Indeed, I could hardly ask for more.

More duck came out, with magic in the whisper of their wings; but none came over me and they were high. All but one lot of six which slipped out late, sharp silhouettes against the rising sun. But the flats were wide and William and I lone specks and far apart.

Gulls started drifting in, great crowds of blackheads, in straggling unregimented wings and columns. A curlew called in the haze, and across the flats came echoing a burst of maniac laughter that told of shelduck wide-awake. Soon a black figure stumbled up from the creek a quarter of a mile away, and William strode across the mud towards me.

"I heard that duck of yours bump from right over there—nice work." He greeted me, "We'd better get cracking on those pits, as it's nearly eight o'clock and the tide'll have us out by half-past nine. That mussel scaup's the place," pointing to a long black scar on the mud two hundred yards out from the dunes. "A lot of stuff collected there on Thursday, and they were coming from both directions, so we might as well stick fairly close together."

That last bit of reasoning seemed a shade obscure, but later it grew clear enough. For I found that lying on one's back it is almost impossible to deal with anything coming from the right. The comfortable arc of fire is only about a hundred degrees left of one's outstretched legs and the maximum very little more.

The scaup, we found when we got there, covered about ten acres, raised a few inches above the level of the flats by the mud that the tides had lodged among the mussels; and as the mud rose, so had they, to keep on top of it. Ten acres of mussels and black mud, cut up and cut again by a network of tiny runnels no one above six inches deep. Between the runnels were level plateaux, many of which held shallow pools whose sides were solid mussel. Little ones, true, but clustered together and clamped so firmly to each other that to pull one loose meant raising a square foot or so of solid shellfish. In all the pools and on all the creek beds lay hundreds of delicate oval saucers, some white and some rose-pink. Shells of the type whose fragments figure so largely in shelduck droppings; only all of these were empty. Live ones, we discovered, live just beneath the surface of the mud, dredging their sustenance from the tides which cover them.

William started work at once. First he drained a plateau of its shallow pool, then marked on its bed at right angles to the shore a coffin shape some six feet long and three across. Facing the sea he started digging along the right-hand edge, piling the spoil along and over the opposite line. Eight inches down he stopped and started levelling the bottom, still piling the dug out mud to the left, till it lay in a ridge whose apex coincided with the original line he'd drawn to mark the left edge of the coffin. Then he cut straight down from the apex through the pile, still throwing the spoil the same way, until the original out-line had become a pit eight inches below the level of the mud with the left-hand wall a further eight above it. Finally he smoothed the inside of the dug out slope till at a little distance it was near invisible—from the left. From the right the cliff edge cut up black enough.

"But the left's the area you'll have to guard, so don't let that worry you," William answered me. "Lie on your ground-sheet with your bag behind your head, and clap a fold of the sheet across your legs to lay your gun in to keep the barrels clear of mud. You might come and lend me a hand with my pit first, though. These clothes weren't made for digging!"

The second pit we dug a hundred yards away, exactly like the first. Only William sited it nearly parallel to the shore, its head towards the other and its feet inclined a little inland, with its cover on the seaward side.

At last it was time to reap the benefit of our work. Odd curlew and godwits, studiously ignored, had passed us while we laboured, so it was with high expectations that I spread my groundsheet and prepared to settle down behind my parapet.

To settle down—that sounds a simple operation. But pit shooting, I soon discovered, holds difficulties not always apparent to the first brief glance; and the greatest of these is MUD. To begin with, your boots are muddy, and there is nothing whatever to wipe them on. The bottom of the pit is muddy, liquid muddy, for the water has puddled somewhat, and the groundsheet settles lovingly into it. You put a hand to lower yourself, and your hand is very muddy. There is nothing to lay your gun on; it touches the pit side, or your boots, and it is muddy. And your muddy hand grasps your gun. A vicious circle. Still, you are in position, and hopefully you fold the groundsheet over your legs to rest your barrels on to save them getting choked with mud. Ye gods, the outside of it is one liquid smear! And in the end a curlew comes. You sit up hurriedly to take the shot, the groundsheet you are lying on rucks up, and the ooze beneath lips over. The picture is complete. Yet people pay good money for mud baths!

I may have wrong ideas of lying pits. In firm dry sand they may be very nice. Or a constant stream of birds may help to counteract that sinking feeling. All I know is, that morning I lay in a jelly-feeling mess for a solid hour and a half till the tide lapped up and made our scaup into an island, and finally a seventh wavelet swept me from my pit. And not a curlew came my way. William got one, the only one we saw.

That seventh wavelet was the end. I struggled to my feet with the pit already half awash, and as I dragged my muddy groundsheet from the welter, from over the sea to my left again came that wretched shelduck's peal of madhouse laughter.

Together William and I waded in towards the sand dunes, trailing our groundsheets in the sea to wash them.

"Luck o' the game," was all he said. "On Thursday that scaup was crowded black with curlew when the tide came up.

9

October 29

All the way down from London the rain had slashed against the carriage windows, and as I stepped on to the platform, a wanton gust of wind whipped round a corner of the station and hurled a handful of icy water straight into my face.

"A rough old night, sir," the station master greeted me; and by the time I'd reached the cottage I could see no reason to dispute so eminently just a statement.

William did not seem pleased with life.

"First time this year we've had anything that looked like decent flighting weather," he remarked at dinner. "I know there are a good few duck in, and some geese, because I've seen them. There's no moon to interfere with a morning flight, and everything in the garden's lovely—except that I can't get off tomorrow morning."

The foxes were the trouble. One had developed symptoms which he didn't altogether like, and he couldn't leave the place in peace until he knew one way or the other just how serious they were. He insisted there was nothing I could do; the car was ready and waiting, and there was nothing to stop me going. Listening to the weather, and having just escaped from its embraces I wasn't quite so sure, but lacked the courage to admit my hesitation.

"I'd meant to try about a mile from where we went down that first day of all," William continued. "You'd do as well there as anywhere, I think. You'll probably find it easier to keep right along the sea wall as far as the culvert —about a mile—then follow out the creek that comes through there. Duck often do the same. Doesn't much matter how far out you go, as they won't lower much till they're right out over the mud and clear of any cover. I generally get as near the mud as possible, to simplify picking up, and occasionally odd birds that have been feeding on the edge fly along it very low. If only the geese were really in this offshore wind would be jammy, but I've seen no weight of 'em yet this year, and the few there are aren't settled enough to be worth planning for."

The wind was still racketing wildly round the house when that cursed alarm went off next morning, and bed seemed even more than usually warm. But mercifully the rain had stopped, and I was brave.

Gun, belt, shells, bag, and boots—I repeated William's formula as I stowed them in the car. Bill, although he was deeply intrigued by these preparations, would not come with me. Doubtless he reasoned that his master might have other fish for him to fry.

I found my way down to the coast with difficulty, for those flat and twisty roads are none too easy for a stranger in the dark. Nor were the saltings, as I soon found out. It was one thing being there in the daylight or with William, but quite another to strike out singly into the black un-known along the top of a bank that might lead anywhere, in the teeth of a gale that felt out the thin spots in my clothing with unerring accuracy. That wide flat coast is an eerie place to be when the wind is howling over it, and I was still too new to the game to realize fully the possibilities of sport that self-same wind might hold. Not very happily, I blundered on.

A shadow on the outside of the sea wall suddenly heaved up and hissed at me, then lumbered off into the darkness with a horrid hacking cough.

I wasn't really scared. Not very. There's nothing really to be frightened of in a consumptive ewe. And after all, they're so completely unmistakable—by day.

How long is a mile? William had said a mile along the wall,

then follow out the creek that ran beneath it, and already I'd spent a lifetime battling into this infernal wind. If I'd missed the culvert I was lost; and rather than face that thought I stumbled on, watching the base of the sea wall ever more anxiously for a streak of extra blackness cutting across the saltings—; and after a bit I found it, to my great relief.

Physical relief as well as mental, for turning my back upon that cutting wind produced a blessed sense of peace. Easy enough to imagine why cattle, caught in the open in a gale, just turn their backs and go on drifting till some obstruction brings them up all standing. Head down and collar up (how I blessed William's rabbit skin) I drifted some myself. The obstructions I met with were creeks, black yawning monsters that gaped horribly, which joined to mine and tried to push me from my course. Always a creek looks bigger in the dark, and thigh boots are not ideal to jump in at the best of times. Still, doubtless the extra effort makes for extra warmth.

Two or three times I put up birds that were roosting in the crabgrass; pipits or finches, small fluttering rags of deeper blackness that struggled for a second before the wind force whisked them off. How did they land and where, those fluttering atoms? The mud was very close, and that was not their home.

By the time the creek I followed reached the salting edge it had grown too wide for comfort, so I hunted for a tributary within easy range of it where I could sit and face the land and still have cover at my back and front. When I sat down, it took me just about a minute to discover that I hadn't stuffed my bag with grass. It does make a difference, that little bit of insulation 'twixt tail and chilly mud.

I was in ample time, for the storm clouds had battened down the dawn; no colours came, just varying depths of blackness as they streaked across the sky. No noises either, the wind took care of that. My flooding eyes stared into it with nothing to assist their search; and nothing crossed their vision, though every nerve was tense with expectation, and it was surely growing lighter. No wings, no disconcerting noise—then a black whisk straight overhead and gone ere I had time to move; I heard them after they had passed.

A movement to the right—low, following the saltings, angling down the wind. A short sharp whistle, just as I swung up to shoot—widgeon, a score or more, and one fell out, far from the bird I shot at, as they flared. The wind whipped off the noise of the reports into a couple of dull flat cracks and I settled down again contentedly, for my victim had fallen on the open mud. A black shape, paddles upward, safe enough. I left him for the moment lest I should miss an opportunity at others coming, for the flight though late beginning now was fairly on.

Bunch after bunch of mallard raced across the stormy sky in lines or shallow Vs, and few so high that they were out of shot. The wind was driving them from dead astern, and they were travelling like bats loosed out of hell; too fast even to climb much at my shots. More and more I longed for William to be there, because most of them were far too good for me.

For nearly half an hour they kept coming, in tens and scores and hundreds until broad daylight had arrived; and even then an odd lot came, riding the gale straight off the land, high up above the saltings clear to the safety of the open mud. Almost as far as I could see they carried on, then turned, and in one glorious set-winged curve stooped down and disappeared.

Two only I had to pick—two and my widgeon. I found the ducks—both small dark birds, the drake's chest nearly black; they never hatched in England. But where was the widgeon? I'd seen him lying paddles up, yet he was gone. I found the place, and the mark where he'd hit and slid along the mud—a tiny blood-stained tuft of feathers—and that was all. No, not quite all—a line of in-toed tracks, the size of a five-shilling piece; he'd walked—and I'd been stung! I followed that line across the mud a hundred yards, and over a sandbank where only the pin-point claw marks showed the way—soft mud again, and down into a creek that wound back to the saltings. There I lost it, nearly a quarter of a mile from where I'd shot the maker. A horrid, empty feeling, but a lesson which has been very useful since.

When shooting solo pick your stuff at once, and damn the cost in chances missed. They're living unpricked birds—

As there was still an hour and a half before the tide was due, I thought I'd try to find out where those duck had gone, so I headed in the general direction where that last lot had curved in and vanished. Patchy going, across belts of mud that sucked and slid away, with worm casts showing black where the surface shone; and over banks of good hard sand, tide-ridged and golden-brown. As far ahead as I could see lay a long black ridge; rather a sharp-cut mussel scaup, I noted vaguely, and thought no more about it. Never a sign of ducks though. Perhaps they were sheltering in some channel; for the wind, though dropping, was still blowing pretty hard.

I must have travelled nearly a mile across the mud, for the sea wall and saltings merged into a single hazy line, and a willow growing out of the bank itself was nothing but a puff against the sky. The mussel scaup was scarcely a quarter of a mile away—a queer-looking mussel scaup, now I examined it more closely. Four or five acres in extent I judged; sharp black, in bold relief upon a rather golden ridge of sand, with a couple of solid looking little outcrops just off the main expanse—

My brain still hadn't registered. Nor did it, till one of the outcrops took wings unto itself and changed into a bunch of ducks which lifted and dropped again into the main black mass. For where they'd lifted from was black no longer, but empty golden sand.

I gaped like any ninny when the truth came home to me—that the scaup ahead was nothing else but solid mallard! The Lord alone knows what their numbers were. Packed close together, black and solid, I'd put the ground they covered down as four to five acres! and when I'd stared my fill my estimate remained the same.

Four or five acres—solid mallard—

Well, I'd found my duck all right. That one bank must have held the population that had come out over several miles of coastline. And it held them safe, entirely unapproachable. No doubt they'd watched me all the way, and decided in their minds exactly how close they could let me come in safety. Even had I known exactly where they were from the beginning it could have made no difference, for all around them the mud stretched almost level, without a creek or any sign of cover. They'd picked their coign of vantage very well.

After a while I tore myself away, for there was no sense in disturbing them unnecessarily. No one could call a morning wasted that had granted such a sight, and it was in a happy frame of mind I headed back into the wind.

Purely by chance I came across the shallow channel where the creek I'd sat in for the flight wound out, and having met it, kept along its edge.

To him that hath … This morning wasn't over yet. I hadn't walked a furlong when I saw them—a long black line that wavered up and down and beat its slow way in towards the land. One look—a rush, and I was in the shallow channel lying on my back. Of course, they might be shelduck. . . . Then across the wind I heard them, and all doubts fled. Geese, fifty or sixty geese—angling towards me—and low, feet only up above the mud.

Lord, but they made a thrilling noise; clearer and nearer it sounded. What did it matter that the wet mud of the creek bed was soaking through coat and sweaters till both shoulders and all my backbone felt the clammy chill of it, if only the creek itself would give me cover.

Thirty, forty, forty-nine, I counted, and all the while their calling grew till I was fairly trembling with excitement, praying to every god I knew. For on their present line they'd pass me very close—

But such beginner's luck was not for me that morning. Whether the old grey gander who led the wanderings of that particular skein had some sixth sense, or whether he just plain mistrusted anything that even smacked of cover I don't profess to know, but within a hundred yards of me, the whole skein altered course and tacked away again across the wind. No fuss, no change of height, no wild alarm note; I do not for one moment think they saw me. But something must have passed from me to them, for as their clamour lessened I felt curiously weak.

Short of the saltings they climbed steeply. I looked for danger underneath, possibly to see one fall. But there was nothing there—only the memory the wise old leader held of former years.

Sadly I watched them as they beat into the wind, a straggling line against the storm grey sky, until their bugle-clamour wavered and was lost—

Back at the cottage I found William much more cheerful, for his patient's symptoms had lessened in the night. Perched on the edge of the steaming bath in which I wallowed, he listened eagerly and rather enviously as I poured out my morning's tale. When I came to the loss of the widgeon he remarked: "At that you got off lighter than one poor devil I took down. With him it was a goose —his very first. It fell in full view, not thirty yards away. Half an hour later, when things had quietened down a bit, he laid his guns down by his bag and went to pick it, and within ten feet of him that goose got up and flew away."

10

November 12—i

The gale had proved a final break-up for the blue October weather. November came in raw and dismal, and for a fortnight London lay beneath a greenish-yellow pall that filtered out the sunlight and drove the city's exudations back upon itself. Soot drifted everywhere and clung to anything it touched. The atmosphere was choking, and leaving it was like entering another planet.

Below my bedroom window at the cottage, the fen lay silent and mysterious; the sky above was dusted full of stars, and above the hill's shoulder a misty radiance marked where the moon would soon appear. This world was quietly sleeping, and I gazed and let its peace wash over me.

I'd come down that evening still a-thrill with the memory of that other morning flight, and confidently dreaming of another like it. William, to say the least of it, had been discouraging.

"Try it by all means if you like," he had told me, "but don't expect to get much. Last time you were more than lucky with your weather; it doesn't look like helping you tomorrow, and the moon's all wrong. We might try a crash round here in the daytime, and in the evening—well we'll see. Tell you what, though," he added cheerfully, "if you're still hopping with surplus energy by bedtime, we'll try a crack of dawn show on Sunday."

However, I'd stayed unconvinced—or obstinate! Why shouldn't I do both mornings anyway? With all those duck about, I'd get a shot or two at least, and easily be back by ten o'clock.

So I went. As I left the car I heard a bunch of mallard winging high out to the mud, though there was nearly an hour to go till dawn. The walk along the wall was easy; so were the creeks, for the moon was still well up the sky, I sat down in the self-same creek as I had done fourteen days before, and waited—and went on waiting. Occasion ally, I heard wings, and sometimes the mallard chattered as they fled, but never a one came close enough even to make me grip my gun. And if they had, I doubt if I'd have seen them. No wind, no clouds, no mist even; three-quarters of a moon shone silver-bright, and the mud was grey and ghostly by its light. The world lay very quiet before the dawn; and she came swift and easily, a crystal miracle of colours. In the east blue faded into green, which paled to lemon yellow—an orange flush, and the sun launched boldly into daylight. Simple enough, but every changing hue a wonder in itself—and all of it was mine.

Out on the mud a greater black-backed gull laughed its hyena laugh, and a drift of hooded crows appeared to quarter down the saltings in search of any unconsidered trifle that the darkness may have left behind.

Idly I picked a stick of samphire and bit into it. It was crisp and salty tasting, not unpleasant; but the mud on it made my teeth grit, so I spat it out. A pinch of white fluff, seed parachute of a sea aster, came drifting on an idle breath of wind. But never a duck, or sign or sound of geese. The only birds of any larder value that I saw at all were shank and curlew, and they were few and distant, for the wader hordes of a month ago had passed.

All the same, I was glad I'd come. William could smile if he wanted—though I doubted if he would—for he had proved exactly right. But tomorrow, I told myself, would see me down again.

On the way back to the car I flushed a short-eared owl, which wafted off on long straight wings that seemed to bounce it through the air. A throng of linnets chivvied it, twittering madly for fifty yards; then frightened by their daring, hurriedly dived back to the shelter of the saltings. A few steps farther, and I stopped amazed. It was just as if some hidden pair of bellows had puffed a bunch of torn-up scraps of writing paper out of the crabgrass a few yards away! A flock of birds, big sparrow size, whose opened wings showed snowy white. They flew with a dipping, finchy flight so that the splashes flickered and vanished, flickered and vanished, then disappeared entirely as the whole flock pitched again.

It was yet another conjuring trick the saltings had produced, and for the life of me I couldn't place them. Twice I followed and put them up again before they tired of the game and flew a mile away, but I never got a real clear view. Some had more white on them than others—one bird indeed was nearly pure; all sorts of varieties I thought of and discarded, but I never touched the truth.

"Snow buntings," William told me over breakfast. "Most years I see some down there. Usually some are pretty white when they first appear—remains of their summer plumage from above the snow-line—but most of it disappears before they've been here long."

It was nearly eleven o'clock before we sallied forth, with Harry, stick and bag in close attendance, and Bill just bouncing with delight. The day had not fulfilled its early promise; light clouds had swung up from the west till the sky was dull and overcast.

"All the better for this evening," William muttered cryptically.

As before, we tried the top land first. But it was a very different picture from that hot September day. The stubbles were ploughed, and the beet all pulled, so that the only cover left was the big old broom and bracken pit in the middle. We saw partridges all right; even more, I think, than we had seen in September. But it was quite another tale to get amongst them. They didn't like the bracken, which though brown, was still waist high; and they did, we soon discovered, like the boundary. More over they flew exceeding fast and far. By dint of much hard walking and not a little ingenuity we finally persuaded two large coveys on to a fallow just beyond the bracken, and sent Harry round by the road to try a drive while we crouched down and waited. One covey split out sideways, but the other came most kindly, slanting across us both. A whirr! a cheerful little call, a yell from Harry. For perhaps three seconds we had partridges in range of us, brown balls of feathered speed; and two remained, the climax of a morning's efforts.

It was a most intriguing morning all the same, of plot and counter-plot—attempted "use of ground and cover "We must have seen a hundred partridges, but never got another shot or looked like doing so. Those birds were truly wild.

There, I think, is the answer to those who claim that partridges should not be shot before October, when they have achieved their fullest strength. Such folk, nine cases out of ten, are owners of big shoots where they have scope to drive and means to see it done. And there, if anywhere, they have the right of it. The birds do fly much better; faster, stronger—farther. Also they are bigger birds when killed. But small shoots haven't got the scope or depth of purse for lines of beaters. Small drives, quiet strategies, may bring odd birds when September and cover are gone. But they are the currants in the pudding of a season's shooting. Without a superabundance of late cover, most small shoot partridges must be collected in September or not at all; for no one cares to shoot paired birds in January, the only other time they are approachable. The coat must be cut according to the cloth. Withal, September walks can be the greatest fun.

After lunch we tried down on the fen.

"Cocks only," William's fiat ran. "They rear just off my boundary so I don't like shooting hens."

In its way the fen showed just as big a change since September as the top land had done. The hedges on its fringe were bare of leaves save where a bramble still clung desperately to some tarnished gold or crimson badge. On the hawthorns clusters of peggles glowed deep red—for the fieldfares had not yet called upon their winter's bounty —but the wild rose-hips were already showing signs of wear and tear where blackbirds and thrushes had torn their glossy covers. On the fen itself the grasses wore a bleached and withered look. Whitely they waved before the wind, for the sap had run back to their roots to wait for spring. Rush clumps showed brown, their seed heads full of black and shining fruit, and along the uncleaned dykes tall reed heads tossed silky manes on stems of fading yellow. Gay colours of the earlier months had fled, and brittle husks remained to face the winter. Even the weeds in the dykes had shrunk and vanished, and through the clear water the rich brown mud below looked deep and soft.

The very feel of the ground was different. In September, the peaty soil had been parched and feather light; now it had soaked the autumn rains up like a sponge and swollen firm again. Although its surface covering might be stale and ragged, the fen beneath was quietly hoarding up a store of wealth against the spring.

In winter, too, the shooting there comes into its own. On cultivated land the game population is pretty stable. So many pheasants, so many partridges you may expect to see and feel aggrieved if they are missing. But the fen land is quite different. Blank yesterday and blank to morrow, today the spongy fields may be full of snipe. Wandering cock pheasants may have strayed along the dykes; a covey of partridges, their stubble gleanings all ploughed in, migrated in search of rush seeds. The water rises an inch or two, and plover, green and gold, flight overnight to search for washed-out worms among the flashes; and in the darkness mallard or teal may do the same, or widgeon come to pull the floating grass blades. Even a woodcock may appear to probe with snipe among the softer places. And any one of these may stay. ... To shoot a fen in winter holds something of adventure.

Beneath a grove of scattered oaks, where the grass was covered with a damp brown carpet of leaves and acorns rolled or scrunched pleasantly beneath our feet. Bill started quartering the ground. His master quietly waved me on to the corner of a rushy field outside—then feathered chaos broke. Four, five, six, seven hens streamed out and passed me; though never a sign of their lordly consorts. But Bill kept hunting patiently and presently he drew away from the trees and down along a dyke; slowly at first, then faster and more confidently out across the open. For us it was a case of run like hell or miss the train—Bill travels when he makes his mind up. We ran, splaying out either side of him so as not to hamper his endeavours. Clear through the rushes to the end of the field he took the line at speed—a cross dyke intervened, and with a fluster and crackle up got two cocks together, bearing across for a wood beyond the boundary.

Both died? I fear me they did not. I ploughed to a standstill, puffing somewhat. I also fired both barrels, though I don't believe they noticed it, for both sailed on unheeding to their sanctuary, checked with a quiver in mid-air and wriggled down between the trunks to earth.

Over the next few minutes I prefer to draw a veil. Bill looked reproachful, William studiously indifferent. I did not feel happy. The tension eased a little when a never-to-be-sufficiently-blessed snipe, which had sat tight during the bombardment, flicked from a dyke out to my left, and died just as I meant him to. Bill under protest brought him back, but plainly he at least was not impressed by such a shoddy substitution.

Nevertheless, it was a start, and from it the afternoon progressed with varying fortunes. Once, when Bill crashed into a reed bed not more than ten yards square, four cocks departed simultaneously, one towards each quarter of the compass. And three of them stayed to keep us company. That was a highlight; we were not always so successful.

One field was full of snipe. Thirty or forty rose and twisted off and never gave a shot. A little owl looped from a pollard willow. William put paid to his account all right, but at the shot five mallard left the dyke a hundred yards ahead. Saving that little owl we should have walked on top of them, for the dyke was deep. Another stern chase after Bill along a dyke towards a hedgerow— the hedge was thick, and we were both one side; the cock got up the other. We tried a long wet stalk-cum-drive to a bunch of plover— but the plover knew a game worth two of that, and offered the dyke we hid in great respect.

Nevertheless, despite reverses the bag crept slowly up; variety at least was there. Teal, pigeon, snipe,—a little owl, a plover— all found their way into William's pockets. Even a bunny, who'd certainly no business on the fen, made an appearance. There was never much risk of our barrels growing hot; but none whatever of our interest flagging. For every bit of ground set its own problems, and every head we got rewarded some small stratagem. Progress alone was none too easy, for many of the dykes had filled too wide to jump, and every field had dykes on all four sides; often enough the only access to it was by a single plank, greasy and half submerged. It was no shoot for the aged and infirm, but we loved every minute, for any minute might produce surprise. Bill pointed at a clump of cover by a dyke—a pheasant, hare, or simply wretched moorhen? Once it was none of these—a small brown bird, swift-winged, flew quick and low and dropped again a hundred yards away. Near as a toucher I shot—a water rail.

The afternoon passed all too quickly. Had William forgotten his half-promised evening's entertainment? We'd have to hurry now to reach the coast by dusk at all. But William showed no signs of haste whatever, and it was growing dark before we turned for home.

As we stopped by a gateway for a cigarette, odd patches of mist were already rising, and a snipe creaked high up in the air. Maybe a wanderer we'd disturbed returning to the fold. Good luck attend his hunting.

"Dry feet for me," said William, shaking himself erect, "the fen's done quite enough for us for one afternoon."

Fifteen head, and eight varieties—with Bill's own contribution of a draggled moorhen, nine. Indeed, she had.

Tea was a grateful meal; and just as we sat down to it... "Look," William exclaimed, pointing to the window.

Not ten feet off a little procession was heading up the hill. Running a few yards—stopping, heads up, tails jerking—running on again. Fourteen partridges. Breathless we watched them, not daring to move a muscle.

Our opponents of the morning; yet neither of us gave a thought to the guns lying across a chair six feet away. Shooting's a funny game!

11

November 12—ii

"Supper's at seven," William suddenly announced while we were cleaning the guns and fighting the day's battles over again before a blazing fire. "That'll give us time to change into coastal kit after, and get cracking by half past eight without unduly straining our digestions."

I sat up with a start. I'd just been getting nicely down to a fore-end with an oily feather, so it took a second or two for the full significance of the remark to sink in. That was what William had had up his sleeve when he talked so disparagingly about morning flights, was it? Stupid of me not to have realized, of course, but I'd so got into my head that dawn and dusk were the times for serious shooting on the coast that I'd quite omitted her lunar majesty from my calculations—save vaguely to condemn her as a hamperer of morning flights.

William would say very little of his plans, but my excitement grew alarmingly when he began to load his cartridge belt; for most of the pockets he filled with BBs and those I knew he kept for one bird only.

"I didn't mean to commit myself," I at last got out of him,

76

"because I didn't trust this sky, and I still don't over much. There are quite a few geese in—just about where you went this morning! At least, there were two nights ago. But if the cloud stays too thick when the moon gets up—ten-ish tonight—they may likely never move at all, and if it clears right off we'll have a job to see them if they do."

The chance of a goose—and tonight! I felt just like a schoolboy on the eve of his first day's shooting. That glimpse I'd had the other morning had been too unpremeditated to savour in advance, but it had proved a very piquant appetizer. My ignorance of geese was only equalled by my anxiety to discover more about them, and for the next two hours I gave William little peace.

"... You see," he told me, "normally a goose feeds by day and roosts at night. But he's a hungry soul, and if he thinks the moon's giving him enough light to find his grub and see enemies by he'll likely go on eating and not flight out at all. Same thing when the moon rises after dark, like tonight. He's gone out to roost already, but if he thinks it's light enough in he comes again at moonrise— and bang goes your morning flight. Leastways, that's the general idea, most any weather variations will alter the details more or less. So will a thousand and one other things— disturbance, food, and so forth—and it's our game to try and get as much of a goose-eye view of current affairs as possible and plan accordingly. It's a chancy business, with a hell of a lot of luck attached to it—but you get your share of thrills if you work for 'em.

"Certainly you'd kill a lot more geese by worrying them on their inland feeding grounds, but you'd miss a lot of fun and end by driving them away. 'Tany rate, it's a game that I'm not playing—

"Tonight? Well, there's no wind to help us, so probably any geese that come will be in the clouds. But you'll hear 'em; and," he added more encouragingly, "there's always the chance that an odd lot may slip in low, especially as they've not been harried down there over much as yet."

Supper—and William's digestion period—seemed hours long, but in the end they passed and we were changed and off. Bill stayed behind, to his most manifest disgust.

"He's had one soaking today," his master said, "and it'd be a long cold wait for him. Besides, the times a dog can do much good after geese are few and far between, and it's astonishing what a noise they make shivering or licking themselves dry when you're listening at full stretch."

It was dark as blazes when we left the car. Much darker than this morning, for there was now no sign whatever of the moon, and the scattering of stars which appeared through a rift in the clouds overhead were not much help in the way of illumination. Apart from that rift the clouds looked dark and heavy, and William shook his head discouragingly.

We cut diagonally across the saltings, and quickly the black ridge of the sea wall merged into the night. Small birds flipped up from the crabgrass as we passed, and once a pestiferous redshank, lurking in a creek on some dark business of his own, did his ample best to rouse the entire marsh. We crossed the big channel after half an hour or so, but William still kept going. As we neared the salting edge the shallow pools we splashed through, left by a later tide, each grew more phosphorescent, till presently every step we took splashed glittering diamonds from the sodden carpet of flattened grasses near the mud.

"Odd how that phosphorescence varies," William remarked. "Some nights you don't see any. We might as well wait anywhere along here. The bank the geese were roosting on is a couple of miles straight out. They've been feeding on some spuds not very far inland, and there's no wind to slant 'em. If they come wide of you, move in towards the first lot and pray the others follow! 'Luck."

Then the shadow which had been speaking turned away and disappeared into the gloom. For a little while sucking footsteps marked its progress, then they were lost as well and I was left alone. The darkness seemed uncannily quiet at first. All the little natural daytime noises were missing, and their very absence drew attention. From out beyond the mud, where the light buoys that marked the channel flickered intermittently, came the throbbing chug-chug- chug of a cargo boat riding the tide into the harbour. Incongruous sound beating on eardrums that tried to shut it out— eardrums that reached into the night, tensed for other sounds entirely. Like a cricket's persistent fiddling, the chugging served to emphasize the silence that it broke.

No signs of the moon as yet, for the clouds had thickened and the rift above closed up. For an hour or more I sat in utter quiet, until the tide came lisping up to fill the creeks and bathe the samphire and sea aster stalks. It was a very gentle tide though, which left the saltings quite untouched and presently drew quietly out again.

Occasionally I heard wings—very occasionally. Sometimes an urgent hissing whisper which made me clutch my gun convulsively, only to realize foolishly when it had passed that only very tiny wings indeed would beat at such a pace. Off to my right a widgeon drake called several times—a long-drawn clear whee-oo that spoke of peace and plenty. And once a mallard, a fat plebian quaack-quack-quack that smashed the salting quiet to flinders and rollicked out across the flats.

But of geese, no sign or sound. Had William dreamed it all, or had they gone elsewhere?

Another chilly hour; it was now long after midnight, and the moon must be well up—if only these blasted clouds would open out a bit. I wondered if William meant to wait till daylight and, despite myself, my thoughts turned bedwards wistfully.

Clouds notwithstanding, it was growing lighter; or may be my eyesight was improving. I could have sworn I saw a star blink over to the west. A moment later, I was sure of it; not one, but several stars, and not just blinking. Like a curtain drawn across the sky, the whole cloudbank had been shifting, and this was the end of it. As it advanced, the moon laid all along its edge a fringe of silver, a fringe which slowly widened. Ahead lay heavy cloud, but all the sky behind was swept and clear and deeply blue, with diamond points of stars.

At last the curtain reached the moon herself, and with her coming the very nature of the saltings changed. Creeks, misty-edged before, took on coherent shape, sharp edged and hard; each dried up stalk of vegetation showed light on the side where the moon's rays touched it, but threw a clean dark shadow to mingle with other stalks and other shadows in a bewildering tracery of black and silver. I sat on the borderline of two quite separate worlds. In front, between me and the moon, each stalk and frond was cut in clear black silhouette; creek cliffs showed solid black, and the wide expanse of mud gleamed jet and silver. Behind, the crabgrass clumps sank into one another, back and back in a single shade of pumice grey, and the mud looked like a misty sheet of gunmetal. There was no life, no colour, in that light, which touched plain honest daytime things into mysterious anonymity.

While I still wondered at the magic change so short a time could bring, there came from the mud a single sleepy syllable—aank!

No doubt whose voice that was, and silently I apologized to William's absent shade.

Ten minutes, quarter of an hour passed, but I knew that geese were out there now, that they would come in—soon.

I waited patiently, without a thought of patience; and presently a confirmation came. Another sleepy note, and a deep-toned muttering that followed. They must have drifted closer on the tide, for that sound never came from two miles out.

Then wings! The slow and solid creak of stiff wide pinions-— too slow, too purposeful by far for any duck. Closer and closer; a low-pitched conversational ang-ang which sounded right on top of me! The moon was very bright, and I stared feverishly—but the creaking lessened and grew fainter, and never a bird I saw.

There wasn't much time for lamentations, though. Out on the mud affairs progressed at last. The muttering grew, swelled to a clamour, then—silence. Suddenly the clamour came again, but with a difference. A moving clamour now; the notes were higher, more distinct and closer, always closer. A biggish lot were in the air, with all bands playing, triumphantly telling the world they were coming!

At that, they were not so foolish. For one end of that skein passed straight above me, yet I never thought to fire. Dim shapes, more visible as a wavering line than individuals, save where the odd bird passed black-limned across the face of the moon herself.

Before their calling faded another lot were in the air. . ..

For upwards of an hour the sky held music. More than once several skeins came in together, and their crashing chorus almost made me drunk with sheer excitement; excitement which the pauses in between served merely to intensify.

Both sides and straight above me, over half a mile of coastline geese came driving in to feed, and with each swelling chorus was the thought that this lot might be low. Small lots and large, most of them quite invisible against the depth of blue; only those that passed well to my right showed clear between me and the rising moon.

If only the sky above would help, even a little. . . .

Twice half-seen half-imagined shadows passed clean overhead; shadows that flicked the stars out as they passed. How high or low they were I could not judge and, hesitating, missed the golden moments, if such they were.

The last lot came—and went. The salting quiet remained unbroken for a timeless interval while anticipation slowly faded and my pulses steadied from that glorious hour.

Splash! Suck! Splash! . . . Astonishing the time that passed between my hearing footsteps and William's actual appearance; and when he did show up he was only a few yards from me. Coming from down moon out of that pale grey background, the moonbeams lent him something of its anonymity. At twenty yards his outline simply melted into it.

"No luck with that first lot," he greeted me, "from where I was they looked to be coming right on top of you. Low, too. Nine I counted, so clearly I forgot for a moment they might be wrong side o' the moon for you to see!"

Together we trudged back to the car. An hour later I was steaming pinkly in a foot of water, with William perched precariously on the bath edge waiting for his turn.

"It was good work on your part not loosing off at those other geese tonight, Rory," he said thoughtfully. "They were too high for certain killing, even with a magnum. But there are so many thoughtless idiots who lose what little self-control they may possess when they see a goose and splash away at him with heavy shot at ranges up to a hundred yards and more, on the off-chance of a stray pellet connecting with the head or neck. Either they never think or just don't care about the suffering they cause by hits in other places. By far the worst criminals are visitors of a type who should know better. Most of 'em would hate the imputation that they took their grouse or partridges at unsporting ranges; yet on the coast their motto seems to be 'There's no one watching, let's take a chance', and a damnably bad and selfish one it is, look at it how you will."

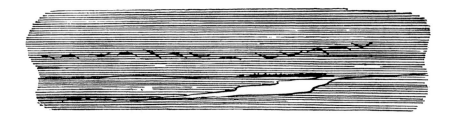

12

November 26—i

In london the fog continued all next week; a grey-green greasy pall. But it lifted with the week-end and the weather bettered; the sky showed blue again, and the night air tingled frosty beneath stars whose twinkling was no longer a matter for conjecture only.

Better, that is, in London. For William's sake I hoped our bane had gone to visit him, for I knew the geese were in, and geese and fog mix well to benefit the fowler.

But before my week-end came the weather clerk produced another change. The wind swung south by west, then west, then north. The sky grew leaden overnight, and before I set out Friday morning a sharp snow scurry had passed a false and fleeting cleanliness over the city streets.

It was raw and damp when I reached the cottage. But the damp was a clean damp, bearing the smell of dead leaves returning to the soil the riches it had given them; and the scent of the wood smoke drifting downwards from a cottage chimney was a pleasant thing. So was the shaft of yellow light from William's open door, and the welcome that awaited me within.

It was quite late that evening when William turned to me and said, "I've something here you might like to cast an eye over, Rory."

I rose and followed him through the kitchen into his little whitewashed scullery-cum-larder. Five shadows hanging from a beam— a mallard, and an old cock- pheasant—but it was at the other three I looked, and looked again. Three grey-white shapes, all mud-bedaubed; long-necked, and long of wing.

So these were geese—. My first thought was "They aren't so very big," but they grew with gazing. That span, those tireless muscled wings!

"All pinkfeet," said William, "and it's a big pink that weighs much above six pounds. This old fellow does by a couple of ounces "— lifting the end bird off the hook that pierced its lower mandible—" He's cleaner than the others too. They fell in the mud and fairly soused themselves. He towered quarter of a mile inland, and I was lucky to get him in the fog, as he was almost out of sight when he upped on his tail and crashed. Bring him into the next room if you want a better look."

It was a nice lump of bird to heft as I took it into the kitchen. All soft mauve greys and browns above, each feather paler edged, and with lighter, grey-white breast. Lord, but that down was thick. I ran my fingers through it and the stiff curled under feathers sprang back into place like wire. The rump was white, with a dark grey crescent just above the tail, and the head and neck were silky with little pointed soft brown feathers that ridged and furrowed lengthwise as I moved the head. The eye, already sunken, sepia brown, black pupilled, and the beak pink banded black, black nailed. At least, the pink had drained to a mauvey, chapped-hand colour where the blood had left it. So had the feet and legs.

Rather sadly I smoothed the feathers. There's always something rather sad about a dead bird in your hand. Half-hidden by the pale grey feathers at the wrist joint of each wing I found a found a small hard gristly spur.

"Ah, I made a bit of a mistake over him," William said. "That spur's not a bad indication of age in a goose. A youngster hardly carries one, but in a real old stager they're often nigh on half an inch long.

"The mistake? Well, a youngster's better eating by far. The theory is that the old birds fly at the head of every skein. In fact, the leader nearly always is an old 'un, but as a goose family is seldom more than five or six there are generally several broods with their attendant ancients in the average skein. Most times— nearly always, in fact— you'll find the leader and the outside birds on each wing are old. Often enough you can see that quite a way off by their size alone. So if you want a bird to eat, and can keep cool enough to think of it, take one, two or three from the outside and never, never take the leader. . . Unless you want a handsome bird to give away, and have a friend you don't much value!"

Sound enough advice, as I've since proved for myself. The snag comes in remembering it au moment critique, when you've watched a wavering skein come in and in, their calling going rather more than slightly to your head. It's a cool hand that thinks of eating qualities then!

My head was full of a chaos of goose thoughts as I clambered up the narrow stairs to bed that night. I'd actually laid my hand on a real wild goose. Somehow that contact had brought the thought of shooting one myself out of the realms of a wild pipe dream into a concrete possibility, almost a certainty. William had slain all three of them in a single morning; the fact that he'd also been out five mornings in the past ten days without a shot paled into insignificance. I'd seen his geese, and held them. That was fact enough. And tomorrow I was going after them myself ... . Imagination quietly drifted into dreamland—

It didn't seem much of a morning when William roused me out. Cold, raw, and freezing sharply. True, there were no stars visible, which argued cloud, but the headlight beams cut two clear swathes that were quite devoid of fog. Still, we were on our way. It was a longish drive, for we were heading for a spot that was new to me.

"Don't be too optimistic early on," were William's instructions as he left me safely embedded in a creek, just where the saltings fringed off into mud. "There's the off chance of a party roosting closer in than usual; the night tide may have lifted and left them. Sometimes a little lot will try to slip in low and quiet before it's light. If you get a sitter at a duck don't pass that up, only don't worry over lesser fry, 'tany rate till well after it is light enough to see what's where. 'Luck!"

Then William was gone, and I was alone, with a rather trembly feeling where my tummy ought to be.

Geese. There might be geese most anywhere around me. So I thought, and resolved that it'd have to be a very persistent duck indeed to tempt me. I firmly turned my back on the land and settled down to watch towards the sea—and geese!

Watch is perhaps a shade untrue, for there was really nothing to see but blackness, as the light buoys in the channel were hidden from my lowly perch by the loom of the sand.

Tide wasn't due till ten; now it was barely half past six —and very, very dark. Also, when the initial flush of warmth engendered by ploughing after William across the saltings had ebbed, I found it very, very, cold. For the wind during the night had backed north-east, and, although it was only a very little thing in winds indeed, it was wearing all its teeth.

Amazing how the darkness lingered. The flight was late as well, for now it was nearly seven, and I'd never heard a duck.

A sudden eerie sighing. . . . Quiet long-winged shapes all around me. Crowding in from the sea, low to the mud, almost on top of me. Hundreds of them, fading into darkness on every side—

Then as I gasped, the nearest saw me. A tiny cry—and they'd flung up and vanished whence they came. It might have been black magic. Only one remained; one, calmer or more curious than the rest, who hung wavering above my head to find out what it was had so put out his fellows. So for a space of wing beats, then he cried softly and flung aside and vanished like a wraith, leaving behind him silence.

But this time not for long. Dawn was nearly here, and between the tidelines night life was giving place to day. More gulls came drifting in on the sighing of a multitude of wings. Thoughtfully a curlew called, far out—and a little trip of dunlins flew low across my creek with a shrill high "skreek" of challenge.

Odd duck were moving out. I heard the guttural ack-ack-ack, and wings a-thrill that marked their passing.

Again a curlew call, which was answered by the ghoul laugh of a black-backed gull. But of geese neither sight nor sound—as yet.

Slowly the darkness lessened. There was no lightening in the east, no picture postcard dawn to watch; just blackness fading into dull dark grey, with heavy clouds low hanging. A bunch of duck swung over and I found that I could see them, so clearly, indeed, that it made me wonder how those earlier birds had passed invisible. Over my shoulder from behind they came, eight coaly specks in echelon—over and out to their day's rest on the sea. I let them pass. In shot they may have been, but not too easy.

William fired twice beyond me, and the reports came dull and flat. Then more duck passed; one pair at least worth powder, but— was I a fool to leave them? The next lot, I decided—

Aangh! Quite quietly, conversationally, to my left. . . . Lord . . . five, six, seven. Angling in, and low, lower than in my wildest dreams. Seven geese, feet only up above the mud—straight in at me.

Where they were heading for I'd no idea. Nor did I care too much. As I clamped right down into my creek they weren't two hundred yards away, and coming. . . .

Right down. For if I couldn't see them it must be mutual. I wasn't taking any risks at all—I thought.

Seconds passed, ages long, and I straightened slowly, very slowly—they should be well in range. . . .

Swoosh, swoosh, swoosh! Ye gods, they were! Almost on top of me. Too close to climb even.... I got one barrel off, and they were past.

Steady, you fool. Stamp around and take your time—they're only feet away.

Stamp round. . . . That creek floor gripped like glue. My foot slipped up inside my thigh boots and I lost my balance.

So low they were that I could see the seven white rumps with their dark grey crescents as the geese climbed after they had passed.

With that little north-west breeze beneath their tails I'd totally misjudged their speed; instead of rising to shoot when they were forty to fifty yards away I'd let them get to ten.

Over the next half hour I prefer to draw a veil. Never in all my life have I felt that life was less worth living. I'd had my chance— and what a chance! and muffed it well and truly.

That little party were the only geese I saw till it was fully light. The rest seemed curiously reluctant to begin their daily feed, and despite myself I started wondering if they'd not departed altogether.

But daylight found them there, a thin black bar a mile or more to seaward. Yet still they simply sat and sat. One little lot did rise, but dropped again. Curiously reluctant they seemed to leave the safety of the mud.

The morning drift of hoodie crows and rooks that had roosted among the pinewoods to the eastward was stringing out across the saltings, quartering the ground. One grey-mantled old scavenger came flopping low towards me, so I got right down in my creek to see how close he'd really come. I'll swear I was out of sight, well down below the crabgrass fringe, yet at forty yards or more the old fox spotted something he didn't like, did a complete back-somersault in the air and fled for dear life along the lane he'd come. It was really a very pretty bit of flying. A quarter of a mile away he lit on a dead old post and croaked his disgust with life to all and sundry. I could see his head jerk down and shoulders rise with the effort of each croak quite an appreciable time before the sound itself got to me.

A sudden murmur from out to sea. Ah! —the hard black crest to the distant sandbanks was dissolving, becoming an irregular moving smudge low down above the mud. Every goose was up and the distant sound of their calling came to me like the smashing of waves upon a shingly beach.

The army circled once, then split; the one half heading up across the flats, and the other—yes—the other was surely coming in. The black smudge clotted and dissolved again, then strung out into long thin lines that writhed and knotted and stretched out as skein crossed skein to fall in for the flight.

Hours they seemed to take, though it couldn't have been more than a matter of minutes in cold fact. And all the time their calling waxed and waned; now dwindling to a few stray notes, then crashing out with the clamour of a thousand throats.

But, alas, they were climbing steadily. Clear between William and myself they passed, in five long trailing Vs. A heavy eight-bore might have fetched them. But I thought of William's words the other week. . . . They made a lovely sight, and a lovely chorus to accompany it, but as an aid to an empty larder the whole show was a total loss.

Inland they passed, safe up above the sea wall, and well inside we saw those wide wings stiffen in a glide towards the earth. Three times they circled, silent while their wings were set, but calling clamorously as they turned or rose a little. Then the leaders dropped behind a scattered fringe of elms, the whole mob followed and were lost to sight.

Out on the sandbank where they had rested three tiny specks alone were left. Pricked birds, most probably, too sick or sorry to keep up with their brethren in the flight.

Well, the game was played. The main chance of the day was done, for the duck were out to sea and all the geese were in. But what a chance they'd given me. Perversely I reflected that perhaps I'd now be happier without that chance.

Two black-backed gulls, a couple of hundred yards apart, came sailing low along the margin of the mud, seeking some slow or wounded bird or just plain offal for their breakfast. I squatted down, for I knew enough of their ways among the moorlands where they bred to detest them for the pitiless murderers they were. But they'd seen me first, and idly altered course a point or two to pass me safely out of range. Slowly they beat on to William's hiding place. Too far out now, I reckoned sadly, to give him any chance.

But I reckoned without my William. From the corner of my eye I saw a white speck shoot up through the air, then fall back fluttering to the mud. The nearer black-backed robber saw it too, for he checked in his flight, and glided straight way over to investigate. He never saw what caused his end. His eager head dropped in mid-glide, and in a whirl of black and white he slumped down to the mud to join the object of his interest.

It was also that of mine by now. Nor had I long to wait. William emerged from hiding and picked it up; also the black-back's corpse, which he brought across and tossed down at my feet. Pink, flashy legs and webs; it was a greater then. Surprising the size of it close up. Standing bolt upright with a foot on one wingtip, I could easily tickle my ear with the other.

"You old serpent," I told William. "How the devil did you 'coy him into you like that?"

William grinned.

"Worked like a charm, didn't it? Here's the answer," producing from his pocket a fine cock widgeon.

If my appearance did me justice I must have looked pretty mystified.

"It's always worth while, if you spot one of those old scoundrels loafing about before he spots you—which isn't often, I admit—and if you've a dead bird on you, especially a light-coloured one, to chuck it up in the air as far as you can. Gully spots it—thinks its a sick or wounded bird and easy meat, I s'pose—and there you are. It'll work two times out of three, provided you're well enough hidden yourself."

"You know," he remarked as we splashed back towards the car, "it might well be worth hanging around a bit down here today. There was something pretty phoney about the way those geese came in this morning. They usually come in bits and pieces starting almost as soon as it's light, and it was nearly eight today before they moved at all—bar your little lot, and you say that they weren't coming in. . . . Anything unusual down here is well worth following up.

"The weather might have something up its sleeve," he added thoughtfully. "They're nobody's fools when it comes to weather propheting. Anyhow, breakfast first, I reckon. We might get Mother Goss to give us some at the Plough—'save going all the way home?"

To be honest, I couldn't have agreed with him more.

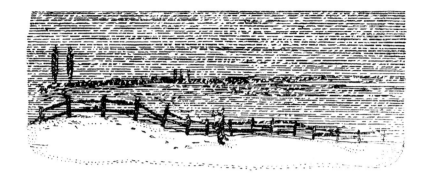

13

November 26—ii

Despite his talk of breakfast it seemed to me that William was steering a pretty erratic course towards it. Sometimes he'd trudge for half a mile in a perfectly straight line across the saltings, jumping or clambering in and out of any creeks that lay across our path; again he'd turn at right angles in towards the sea wall, then parallel it, or without a word slant out across the saltings on another leg.

As the crow is alleged to fly, the car wasn't a couple of miles away, but William's zigzags must have added half as much again. For a while they puzzled me almost to the point of remonstrance. Then I noticed that every leg brought up at a patch of short grass bare of any cover, which usually enclosed one or more little salting pools; and these and their surroundings William studied carefully in passing.

I held my curiosity till we were well on with our break fast. William's not over fond of damn fool questions on an empty tummy.

"Widgeon droppings," he told me, when at last I asked what he'd been searching for. "Droppings, and nibbled grass to show where they've been feeding. It's a shade early yet, as we've had no weather for forcing 'em to feed on the saltings. But moonlight widgeon flighting to my mind's so much the most thrilling of all the salting amusements that I'm not overlooking any bets I can help. You see, most widgeon hereabouts feed on ordinary green short grass—there's little enough zostera round this bit of coast, and with the snow or floods their inland grazing's often covered and they're forced down to the salts.

"Then, if you're lucky and know your spots, and get the moon right, and the sky right, and the tides right, and the weather right, you may, if you're lucky enough to get the saltings to yourself, achieve a night of nights. Or you may not. Widgeon have a magnificent knack of having been the night before to the spot you choose, and only a few stragglers arrive the night you go. It's a great game though. More than any other, I think, it keys you up and keeps you mentally a-tiptoe every second, and once you've heard widgeon calling as they flight into you under a half moon and a cloudy sky, I dare prophesy it's a sound you'll never have enough of."

For the remainder of our breakfast, I gave William little peace, and the talk was widgeon, widgeon, widgeon. I learnt that although some nested in the north of Scotland and even a very few in England, the great weight of the widgeon round our coasts were winter visitors, and that a cold spell on the Continent increased their numbers beyond all recognition; in the winter they are our commonest wild duck, but for every one seen inland there are probably ten that spend the daylight on the river estuaries and sand banks out to sea; that where they were harried most of them didn't flight till after dark, though early in the season they often fed by day as well as night; that the drakes, especially the youngsters, were often very late in donning their full plumage, and sometimes it was well on into February before they reached their full cream-crested glory; that they responded well to calling—if you were cunning; and over and above all that the sound of a cock widgeon calling in the moonlight was the greatest thrill the saltings had to offer.

These things and more he told me, while Mrs. Goss plied our appetites with a truly gargantuan breakfast of eggs and toast and sausages and bacon; and later, as we smoked our pipes of peace and gently steamed before the fire. Stale news to most folk, probably, but most of it to me was fresh and more than interesting.

"Ten o'clock." William looked at his watch. "Tide'll be turning in half an hour or so. If the weather's going to pull a fast one, according to local lore it'll likely do so with the change of tide. So we'd best get cracking."

I shivered as we left the pub. Mother Goss's fire had been so very warm and pleasant, and outside that thin little wind seemed to have grown even thinner.

Where we left the car the surface of the track was powder dry, and the ribs between the cart ruts along its edges were frozen hard as flint. Tide was well in; a restless grey brown stain that covered half the saltings. We split and wandered out across them with no fixed aim in view. Occasional little parties of knots and dunlins flickered along the cream splashed tide rim, like moving foam flecks as they turned their breasts towards us. The ubiquitous redshank screamed derision as he fled.

Right to the waters' edge we went and there knelt down. Already they were ebbing, for a rim of brittle ice cakes marked the limit they had reached. Ice cakes made up of the freezing skim of water the tide before had laid above the mud. This, frozen in the bitter air, was floated by the ensuing tide; floated in tiny scales and spicules, pushed up ahead like foam by the early waves, and piled, cake upon muddy cake, a long high-water mark. There, cemented by the water which splashed over them and froze, they slowly formed a tiny barrier reef of rotten ice.

In the creeks the small floes rustled and crushed together as the outflow jostled them; some stranding, some journeying on the muddy current to bob about at sea until the next tide brought them in.

If this cold lasted the waders would get slim pickings for the next few days. Already it seemed to me the knots were more restless even than their wont. More restless, and less wary, for they took singularly little notice of the two very obvious bumps that were William and myself. Indeed, as far as William was concerned, I noticed several lots go out of their way to pass in range of him. Surely he couldn't be calling them? What sort of noise did a knot make anyway? All I'd ever heard from them was the rush of their wings and on occasion, a tiny guttural croak that was quite inimitable.

When the sea was clear of the saltings half an hour later we foregathered and I asked him. Between us we'd seventeen knots and one grey plover which I'd shot from among a score or so of knots that flew low past me.

"You're right, I was trying to talk to them," William admitted. "It's curious, but little lots like these will often come quite nicely to a whistle. Though Lord knows what they think is calling them unless it's a grey. I've never heard knots whistle, but often enough you see them with grey plover. There may be some connection." He pursed his lips and gave a high clear whistle, a liquid double note, "That's all I do about it," he said. "Some days they'll come…".

William was gazing fixedly towards the land. Away inside the sea wall, in the direction the geese had disappeared, stood a cluster of wind-starved elms; to their right the bare steel structure of a wind pump, whose groans as the increasing wind pushed up the revolutions of its fan were audible even from where we were. Caught between gusts it had a deceptively goose-like note. . . .

With these two bleak exceptions the green line of the sea wall stretched unbroken as far as the eye could see; a cut between frost-bound earth and a sky that was heavy with its burden.

Even as I watched, a grey-white curtain swept across and blotted out the elm-clump.

"Here she comes," William cheerfully remarked. "Better split up—'bout as we were before. One never knows."

After due reflection, I fancy that he'd more than a suspicion though. . . .

Before I reached my creek two hundred yards away the snow was already beginning. A dry little gust of wind that carried with it small cannon balls which it flicked spitefully into eyes and face and ears. Hard little balls that cut and stung and bounced off to the ground again; not hail, yet not entirely snow.

Brrh! I crouched down under the shelter of the over hanging obione clumps that fringed my creek and wished most heartily that my rabbit's skin collar had been a polar bear's.

Then the geese came—; and the sight drove every thought of cold discomfort headlong from my mind. In truth, it was a sight I shall not easily forget. Fully three thousand of them, William said, came riding the vanguard of that storm from off the land. The sky was crossed and criss-crossed with their skeins, and the music of that crying horde merged into one continuous paean.

Straight over me some passed; straight above William others. And over all the half mile stretch that lay between us. Straight over, out to sea, and glided set-winged till the snow wreath hid them from us.

They'd been too high, of course. Too high by far. But somehow that hardly seemed to matter. The spectacle they had shown us made almost sacrilegious the thought of cold grey bodies hanging by the neck.

And yet—there was challenge in their calling; in the easy scorn with which they passed us by. And I knew that I had taken up their gage; that henceforth I would follow them, perversely seeking to break through their proud indifference which thrilled me to the very marrow of my bones; and that the only outcome of that chase would be their death. It was a funny muddle. I loved them, yet I sought their end—though that alone was not the end I sought.

Strange thoughts for the position I was in. A slippery muddy creek; a bare bleak salting; a whirling snowstorm in November.

For now the snow was falling heavily; the small crisp pellets had changed to great white fluffy flakes that clung to the rough tweed of my jacket and settled meltingly behind my ears. Visibility was limited to a hundred yards at most.

Withal, it was not so cold. The weight of snow had killed that biting wind, and without it life was easier by far. Besides, there was something vastly comforting in the thought that the geese were out. For they'd have to feed, and to feed they'd have to come in once again, which meant that we'd get a second flight, and that in broad daylight. While snow was a state of affairs that William prayed for when there were geese about—

Out on the sandbars those geese were now.

I began to wonder. Each night they went out there; somewhere out there. Between the tides in daylight, too, at times, a-gathering sand to help their gizzards grind their food. Was it the same bar they used each time? If so, why shouldn't we forestall them, and dig a pit to wait for them out there? Tides would want watching maybe, but the birds themselves would surely be right low—The more I thought, the more I liked the possibility. Why hadn't William thought of it before?

Meanwhile the snow continued. Inshore the saltings were a

white expanse which merged indefinitely into a thick white curtain of falling flakes. Even on the tide ridges of the frozen mud the snow lay white. And the geese appeared to have no desire at all to leave their distant sandbanks. For over two hours, I sat there and never heard a sound.

A solitary dunlin, fat and fluffed up, ran busily along the lip of the creek within ten feet of me. Little short run, then dip and probe and hurry on again lest he should miss the tiny morsel which his body needed. He was a friendly little soul; I missed him when he flitted on with a small shrill "scree" to search for fresher pastures.

Then through the white curtain geese came calling. At last. I knelt forward, flattening against the opposite over hang of the creek. Hell, but the patch where I'd been sitting looked dubiously black and free from snow!

It wasn't a big party that was coming—so I judged— but they talked incessantly; and—surely there was a note of doubt about that calling that I hadn't heard before? Less confident—anxious almost—it sounded to my ears; but closer, closer yet—and still I couldn't see them. . . .

Blazes! But they were moving to my right. The calling rose and fell, invisible—but alas, it was surely growing fainter.

Boom! Boom! Then silence. The reports came muffled, but William's they must have been. Then I heard geese again, fainter and fainter, till they too were silent.

Hell and damnation! Why hadn't they come to me. For a moment I felt almost sick with pure jealousy.

Then I remembered. Only this morning—those seven shapes almost on top of me. The fates that rule the fore-shore don't easily relent towards a duffer. Besides, for William it was the first chance of the day. Somehow I never doubted that he must have scored.

But there were still geese out there.

A half-hour's wait, and then another little party moved. Again they passed in to my right and again the snowflakes hid them from me. But they didn't go right in. I heard them turn and swing along the saltings, and presently drift out to sea once more. This time I was sure their calling did not sound so confident.

Then, suddenly as it had come, the snowstorm cleared. Invisibly the heavy clouds had thinned and drifted past, and in a matter of minutes the sun broke dazzlingly through to strike a world so swept and clean that its white ness almost hurt. Saltings, sea wall, even the distant trees and wind-pump, had been touched by magic, sparkling clear; while the powder blue of the sky scouted the very thought of dirty weather.

And to seaward—ah!—there they were. That thin black bar right out beyond the pearly gleaming mud— geese, geese, geese. Even as I watched, the sunlight touched them too, and the quality of its light cut the black bar down to half its thickness. Grey backs and bodies merged in with the grey mud flats where the sunlight struck them. It was the substance that stood invisible while the shadow grew hard and clear. Their backcloth was the snowstorm, white drifts on heavy grey.

They didn't keep us waiting long. Almost at once the first lot jumped. The small dots knotted and unstrung, tangled and fell back into line as the skein came calling in.

Calling. No sound of hesitation in that joyous bugling now as the V swept on and inwards. Nor in the manner of their flying as they climbed.

It was the old, old tale. A gunshot and a half above me they came over; each pinion etched against the frosty blue, each breast reflecting the flung back radiance of the snowy ground.

Before they'd passed the next lot were a-wing; then more and more. In thirties and in forties and in hundreds they came crying in, and for half an hour the transformed saltings were glorious with sound.

William's judgment had been sure enough once more. We were squarely in their line, but never a shot we fired. For a while we watched them circling right away inland; odd bursts of calling drifted out to us. Their feeding grounds had altered—they didn't altogether trust them. For a time I prayed they'd come on out to sea again. But hunger conquered caution, and the first lot were down. Soon all had dropped behind the trees and the silence settled down once more.

A small black figure in the sunlight—William.

Stiffly I levered myself up from my hiding and scrunched across to meet him.

Sure enough, the mudstained canvas of his game bag showed

a comfortable bulge. Of course, it might be crab- grass— But it wasn't. I peered inside. A pink-footed goose, the flesh tint of its beak already draining pallid, throwing the black nail and nostrils into even clearer contrast.

"'Bout forty of them," William told me. "Just blundering around, they were. It's odd how foolishly a goose'll often act in snow. They seem to lose their way and wits as well."

He glanced at his watch. "Doubt if it's worthwhile staying for the evening flight. Sharp frost tonight, from the looks of it. With this clear sky we'd have a job to see a duck. 'Tany rate it'll be damn near teatime when we do get back, and I'm beginning to want my lunch!"

Three o'clock, just on. Five hours simply magicked past in weather I should hitherto have regarded as only fit for lunatics to venture forth in. And in that time a single chance at geese between us! Truly this coastal game had points.

Full fed, and warm, and blissfully relaxed before a blazing fire, I tackled William about trying for the geese out on the sandbars.

For some time he was silent. Then—

"It has been done, of course. But I don't think you'd ever get. a local gunner trying it. One of the professionals at Wells told me of a party of 'furinners' who came and dug in out on the roosting bar there. His story, without trimmings, was that although they did get a goose or two they cleared that stretch of coast for the best part of a season. And I've no cause to doubt him.

"Say, for instance, you dug in where those geese came out today. You saw them go out for yourself, in one or two big lots. So that the most you could expect to get would be a couple of chances. Gifts, maybe, if all went right. But the price you'd pay for those two gifts would be to scare, and scare badly, every single goose on that stretch of coast. Birds'll stand quite a lot of harrying on their flight lines, but quiet to feed and sleep they must and will have, or they'll drift elsewhere in search of it.

"I don't say that they would shift after one attack. But I'd hate to say they wouldn't, and it'd be a singularly selfish trick to try."

14

DECEMBER 4

All the early week the snow kept falling, while I sat and savoured one of the bitter-sweets of wildfowling. For once you begin to know a strip of coastline, and have striven hard and unavailingly with the inhabitants thereof under weather conditions which give them every advantage, and then for a brief moment the fates relent and send a spell which may give you a chance; afterwards, wherever you may be, that weather spell has only to repeat itself to take you back in retrospect to your strip of coast, with the ducks or geese or widgeon behaving just as they were that other day of snow or fog or sleet. Only now the difference is that you're inevitably beneath them—they're coming low, all round you, almost too fast for you to load. Whereas on that day, perhaps—well, if only you'd been just a little farther over...

And now I'd ten more days before I could even hope to see the coast again, and our climate is notoriously unstable. Ten days to sit and suffer...

It was Wednesday when I got William's postcard: "Come this weekend in place of next. I think we might have fun."

Despite my almost tearful plea, the office couldn't let me go. To be fair, it was a busy time for us. And Saturday, four-thirty, was too late for the last train down to William.

Despairingly, I rang him up and told him of my woes, but he made light of them.

"There's a late train through to Scotland," was the reply I got. "I'll meet you at Peterborough at seven. You can change in the car and we'll be down on the coast soon after eight which mayn't be too far out. It may be all a false alarm, 'cos it's purely guesswork on my part, but I'm hoping that with this melting snow some of the inland feeding widgeon may be flooded off their feeding grounds and forced down to the saltings. 'Tanyrate we'll see. There's just on a full moon." And clack! went the receiver before I'd time to ask a single question!

So much for my ten days' suffering! I could hardly contain myself till Saturday.

Peterborough station—and there was William and the ancient motor. Apart from a jacket and an outer pair of flannels I was changed already.

Gun, thigh boots, canvas bag, cartridges—William had them all there waiting for me. Mainly short sixes in the shell belt, I noticed—the shiny lacquered ones—with half a dozen three-inch BB's in the usual place. Oh Lord, but this was good.

The moon was hanging clear of cloud as we left the town behind us; a smoky lemon disc not 45 degrees above the flat horizon to the east.

"We shan't do badly with the time," William said. "There'll be a biggish tide just emptying when we get down. That may mean a few birds scattered feeding where it's left the grasses wet, but fresh water in the flashes should be a big attraction. We'll visit one or two of the larger ones and if we put away any weight of birds we'll wait an hour or two to see if some return.

"As I told you on the 'phone, I know nothing, and this is a chancy game at the best. But conditions might be a whole lot worse. If only it'd cloud up a bit."

Down at the sea wall once again. Squeeze into thigh boots. The smell of the salts hung keen and tang on the night air. Not too warm either, it seemed at first. The dyke banks on their inland side still wore collars of drifted snow, though even by moonlight these looked worn and dingy, and outside on the saltings no trace of white remained.

Eastwards into the rising moon William set off.

"One word of warning," he flung over his shoulder. "Even if we find stuff on the flashes and get close enough, don't shoot. It'd probably scare 'em right away for the night at least."

Flashes? What were these flashes William kept talking about? Then I thought of the little pools set in the patches of close green turf we'd visited the other day. Tiny crab-haunted pools, cliff-sided, six or eight inches deep. Only somehow they didn't seem quite to fit the bill.

They didn't—altogether. William stopped presently at a patch of close-cropped green right enough; but the little pools it held had been overfilled and flooded into a single shallow pan of water that merged and seeped among the grass roots so that a patch ten yards and more across was half submerged and splashy.

"H'm. Nothing do here." William bent down to look more closely round the water's edge. "We'll wander on a bit."

Then out of the darkness came a short clear whistle. Another— and another, joined to a deep dry purring croak. Wings, swiftly swelling—urgent—then sadly dying. Another short clear call and they were gone.

Oh, but it was a thrilling noise.

"One little party on the move, anyhow," muttered my guide. "There's another good flash to visit half a mile farther on, and we might as well both wait there to night."

Half a mile farther on— How the devil William finds his way about these saltings in the dark beats me. The view on all sides looks identical; but I suppose it's a case of each cock to his own dung-hill.

At any rate, here we were— I heard them, as they rose. Almost I thought I saw them flicker past the moon, but it was that chorus of whistling and sighing wing-beats that fairly took my breath away.

" 'Bout a hundred at a guess," William informed me. "Lord knows if any will come back tonight, but it's well worth waiting, for they weren't scared badly. There's no wind to speak of—or cloud either, worse luck—but if we sit down fifty yards apart this side of the flash we should get anything dropping in below the moon and see it more or less. You'll find a little creek you can get your legs in, and if you keep your face down nothing will see you sitting still."

That creek was most convenient. It ran along not ten yards from the water's edge, so I stuffed my bag with crab-grass and sat me down in comfort. This was de luxe. Nice, warm, dry night (after our half hour's walk); dry seat, no mud. What more could the heart of man desire? Widgeon? Ah I settled down to take further stock of my surroundings.

Behind me the crabgrass stretched grey and misty in the moonlight. My creek was a clear-cut line of demarcation, for in front was that lovely close-cropped-looking salting turf. A lawn at least a hundred feet across that reached off to my right, past William, till I lost it in the loom of the sea wall. And down its centre, twenty feet away, a splash of water curved from him to me. As I stood up, the moonlight rippled yellow from its surface, for although there were no clouds, there was none of that frosty silver in the night as yet.

Below the moon—a black shape that see-sawed bat like from side to side—was it really? ... and even before I could clear my eyes a shot rang out, my bat shape slurred, grew heavy—splash! And the first widgeon of the night was down.

Blast! but he'd come in quietly—and alone. I must keep more awake.

William was out there picking up at once.

Ten minutes later the same scene was repeated; only this time I'd never even glimpsed the bird, which splashed even more in front of me than the first! No noise, no wings, no nothing. Singleton widgeon, slipping in to pitch.

From farther along the saltings came a long clear whistle. A couple of minutes' pause, then from the same direction it came again. A widgeon drake, all right, but how very different from the short sharp urgent calling of the drakes in the party that had passed along before! This placid call seemed to tell a tale of peace and plenty.

Right at my elbow came an answer, startlingly loud—the same long thrilling notes. Feverishly I stared at the flash. This time he must have slipped in without either of us noticing, a thought I found exceeding comforting! And I'll swear it wasn't till I heard him chuckle that the truth sank in—William had made that second call himself!

Presently the cock bird called again, and William answered him. Then once more wings—and a chorus of short clear pipes. William spoke only twice.

A blur of black shapes over me, absurdly fast across the stars. I straightened, for at their noise I'd crouched—quite needlessly—down almost double! And to my shot one black shape slumped, grew clearer, heavier—crashed. The rest fanned up and promptly vanished into darkness. Yet William got a double shot and picked another bird! Don't ask me how he saw them with that sky behind!

My very first moonlight widgeon was lying there on the salting grass before me. A drake, moreover, which was pleasing. Somehow it always seems more satisfactory to pick a cock bird and especially with ducks of any sort!

Three hours more we waited, while the moon grew higher and more silver, and details on the ground showed up so very clearly it seemed impossible that anything could pass us by unseen. Yet time and again we heard wings or calling that made us strain our eyes into that deep blue sky, mouth open, breathless, tense; and several times I know they were in range, yet even William failed to pick them up. Odd shots we did get, though, with varying success, and by midnight we had seven birds between us.

"And," said William, as we strolled back to the car, "I've been whole seasons 'fore now without a better night than that, so we've little enough to grumble at."

Grumble, forsooth! I was still tight keyed-up with excitement when I tumbled into bed. William once more was wholly right. Moonlight and widgeon whistling; there's magic lurking there.

Next morning, I saw his call. It was a home-made job, built from the brass ends of two 8-bore cartridges after the fashion of those suck-and-blow tin horrors one used to find in crackers at children's parties. The caps had been punched out, and one case driven hard inside the other. The result, when played right, was certainly astonishingly real.

"'Taint so good as a well-done natural whistle," William told me, "but that's an art I find is quite beyond me. Even with this, if you don't overdo it, a widgeon is worth calling to at times; well worth it."

15

December 5

Next day from early morning we were busy handling foxes. Catching, examining, combing and comparing some of the most lovely living furs I've ever had the luck to see. The brunt of the pelting was over, and William was reduced to sorting out the last half dozen to be killed that year—the borderline cases—from those he considered good enough to keep for breeding from the following season. As he said, "It costs as much to keep a bad fox as a good 'un, and a bad 'un won't breed good, so why not keep your best?"

The trouble appeared to be the picking out. If I'd been a girl there wasn't a one of those beauties I wouldn't have been proud to wear. By two o'clock, though, we were through and for six of the foxes we had handled the fates had called.

"Lunch now," said William, "and then we'll get right on down. Harry can feed. I want you to see those widgeon spots by daylight—and so do I."

At half-past three I was standing by my last night's pew. Rather stamped about it looked by daylight, where I'd tried to kick myself a seat in the creek side.

"Untidy of you." William nodded to a dozen empty cartridge cases lying on the grass, "Always pick those up and stamp them into the mud of some creek bed. You see, you're up agin' the other man as well as the birds in this game, and it's no use advertising where you've made a killing. 'Sides, I'll warrant most of the 'regulars' know each other's brand of cartridges and can hazard a pretty good guess as to what the empties mean."

By four o'clock the sky was clouding over nicely. With any luck the moon would be entirely hidden. Tide would be full by five— fairly big, but without a wind to back it, not reaching far up on the saltings. It was still increasing with the moon.

And then I wondered—those flashes? The tide could not have covered them for upwards of ten days, and they were noticeably smaller even than last night. At that rate they should have emptied in two or three days at most.

"Snow water," William told me. "Heavy rain some times, but snow's your likeliest bet if it'll lie, and then thaw quickly. Then, and after the very biggest tides, are the only times you'll find the flashes full. You can see there's been a fair few widgeon feeding by this one the last few nights," he added.

All round the puddle's rim short bitten-off ends of grass were floating in an oily scum and the bordering turf, wherever the water had covered it, was ragged and pulled about as if it had been thoroughly teased with a hay rake. Everywhere there were droppings, bright-green, white-tipped and about as thick as a lead pencil.

"Widgeon, all widgeon work," William muttered. "And recent too. Here's your everlasting problem cropping up again. Do we wait here tonight and pray they'll come again, or do we try another flash and hope we've guessed ahead of them?"

Finally we decided to copper both bets; William to try a fresh pool farther on while I was to pray that last night's visitors returned! But for the flight itself we would try the tide edge in the hope that an early bunch or two might skim along it.

With this plan fixed, William lurched off towards the setting sun.

Already the waters were lapping up the little creeks, gurgling happily as they swilled into the empty cracks and crab holes, their vanguard bearing bravely with them bubbles and flecks of foam and the lighter debris that goes to form a normal high-water mark. Soon I was driven from my cover and kneeling in the open. Not that it mattered much, for it was dusk already and a bird would have to be very low indeed to get me silhouetted.

There were the first of the duck—I heard them chattering well before I picked them up. No fear of them being low enough, although I had loaded with three-inch fours for the flight. Nine, ten, eleven, in they went—a line of coal-black fragments against a ragged-edged grey shawl of cloud. Gazing at it, I reflected that it almost looked like wind to come—those harried looking strips—ack-ack-ack-ack! Eyes to your front, fool. Three of them this time—nigh low enough as well. I heard the pellets rattle as they flared, but the second barrel took the leader fairly in the crop, and for a moment my heart raced madly in sheer joyous gratitude as he crashed earthwards. And although I says it as shouldn't, it was a pretty shot. Then an old curlew fooled me nicely, just to restore my mental balance.

More duck came in, but never gave another chance. The tide lapped round my knees continually and forced me back. It was getting dark, too, but still I could see quite clearly birds that I'd never have glimpsed last night, despite its brilliance, although the moon could hardly be above the flat horizon yet.

Widgeon! The jumble of short clear notes from out at sea cut straight through any other thoughts. Insensibly, I stiffened, listening. They were on the move, but not to me.

Back to my flash, or wait here for a while?

I waited on the tide edge for an hour, in the end moving as it moved, till the waters went back home again. And for nearly all that hour I heard widgeon, out to seaward.

Two parties of a score or so came racing past me, and from the second two birds fell to my first barrel, twin splashes in the shallow water. I strode to pick them up.

Hell! I was on my face, both thigh boots full, gun, arms and chest, all spread-eagled in the muddy water! I knew it was shallow enough, but had clean forgotten how perfectly it would cover up and hide the creeks.

Praise be, I had kept my barrels upwards as I fell. They both showed clear of mud when I glanced apprehensively through them towards a lighter patch of cloud. But my widgeon? Where on earth were they? For every direction looked alike to me.

Lord, but I mustn't lose them now. Heartsick, I tramped and splashed, circling outwards from the place I'd crashed. Quarter of an hour later I caught the gleam of a white tummy where one had stranded upside down against a tall sea aster stalk, and felt grateful. The second bird I never found.

The search had warmed me up, but I was parlous wet, and as the tide had left the saltings I retired back to my flash.

There was a lovely sky. All dark-grey, patchy clouds with light between where the light from the rising moon struck through them. To be sure, things on the ground were wholly indistinct compared with last night—but just let those widgeon come again.

Only they never did. Not a single bird, although I sat there shivering till eight o'clock was long since past. After those early ones at sea I never even heard a widgeon, though odd mallard kept flighting inland till close on seven. A little wind was rising too. Only a little one, but it struck clammy cold through my wet clothing, so that I wasn't sorry to hear William coming to collect me, for I'd sworn to myself never to approach him first.

"Incalculable blighters, aren't they? I got a couple early on the tide. You got one and a mallard too? Nice work. It's hardly worth waiting any longer.

"I reckon they'll be at their supper by now, wherever that may be. I'd give a bit to know, 'cos I made sure we'd get a crack or two tonight."

16

December 26

"Boxing day shoots. Aye, by and large, there's more real keen enjoyment got out of shooting on Boxing Day than in any other six days of the year, I'd say. Unorthodox some of the parties may be, but— Look here, if you've nothing particular on over Christmas and would like to spend it with my folk over in Herefordshire, I'll introduce you to one of the more original brands if you like. I don't think you'll find it dull, whatever else."

Thus William, and beyond that slightly sinister utterance he refused to commit himself.

Now Christmas was only a fortnight away, and my luck in the leave hue had been clean out. I'd only got a couple of days, which didn't admit of any very ambitious programme, so the suggestion fell rather as manna from heaven.

William, however, stayed singularly reticent as to the exact form his Boxing Day entertainment was to take, and the morning itself found us crossing the border into Welsh Wales with me still little the wiser.

In the back of the car were our guns and about 150 shells apiece—but no dogs; and that was curiouser and curiouser.

The weather for once was truly kind, for the day was of that blue white that follows hoar frost, and the twisty lanes wanted watching at the corners. We drove through some lovely country; red plough and bright green pasture climbing up to the russet bracken which bordered on the deep brown of the moors above; thick well-kept hedges in the valley, growing progressively more open and straggly as they climbed, till they dwindled and vanished into ragged grey stone walls on the moorland's edge; through stone-built, slate-roofed villages whose walls were spotlessly colour-washed in shades of pink or cream or white. Everything looked blissfully quiet, peaceful and permanent after the rush and scurry of a spell in town.

Presently the road twisted down and down into a wide shallow basin in the hills, and with a bump we left it to follow a winding track across a field right to the edge of a wide reed-fringed lake that covered the basin's floor.

Although it was only ten o'clock, there were already upwards of a score of people there, clustered round a rough old wooden landing stage to which was moored a very motley collection of dinghies of all known shapes and sizes; ranging from a venerable family 8-seater with a girth proportionate to its responsibilities, down to a rakish home-made affair with outriggers painted a singularly revolting shade of green. The guns were a mixed looking lot, too. A party of "city sports" stood by themselves, pump-gunned and befeather-hatted, talking loudly—and big; but the large majority were local farmers and their dependents, with a scattering of tradesmen from the nearby towns. They were as friendly a gathering as you could wish to meet—all out for the one idea, their "bit o' sport". William was received with a cheery hail, and a good deal of back-chat about the straightness or otherwise of his powder.

"Curious kind of cartridges I've got this year," he answered unexpectedly, loud enough for the city folk to overhear. "Sort of touchy—if they hear a shot whistling about too near, they're apt to answer back and go off like of their own accord."

"Bit touchy on that subject yourself, aren't you, mister?" an old farmer answered with a twinkle, and William laughed.

A chorus of "Here comes David," and a temporary pause to the general chatter, for David the boatman was regarded by every one as the ex-officio Master of Ceremonies. He made his living in the summer by letting out his boats to all and sundry and was a mine of information about the lake and the best holes and bays for perch and pike. He soon got everyone sorted out into the various boats.

"Yess, yess, plenty of coots this year, plenty of coots whatever," he told William as he shoved us off in the Alice Emily, a vintage dinghy built "to carry 4".

"Coots?" I looked at William—surely we weren't going to shoot coots? I had always looked upon a coot as a sort of superannuated waterhen, with much the same powers of flight, but all the satisfaction I got was "Wait and see ". William at times was simply maddening.

As we left the landing stage I got a better idea of the lake itself. This was about a mile and a half long and perhaps a mile across, shaped roughly like a fat stubby letter "L", with the stage at the outside of the angle, and a little island, which supported a flourishing tribe of goats, just to its left. Almost the whole shore was fringed with reeds, a belt of a hundred yards or more in depth from where the water's edge had stood in summer. Only now it was winter, and the surface of the lake had spread. As William put it, "Seen from the hills above, floods make the lake look far more like the top of a bald and tonsured head than is altogether decent". But from water level this suggestion was mercifully not apparent, and the view was altogether lovely. On every side the green full-hedged fields ran gently up from their reflections into little wooded dingles which twisted up into the bracken and the moors above. The fields and hedges held single trees that had been left graciously to glory in a quiet old age. Mirrored in the water was the reversal of the tiny grey-stone church which stood on a promontory above; while behind it, half hidden in a wood, a cluster of snowy cottages marked the village which it served.

A legend has it that in olden days the village had stood on the floor of what was now the lake. But the people had been a wicked people and the floods had been sent to cover the village as a visitation for their sins. Even now, the story said the old church bell could be heard tolling its warning from beneath the waters. If the legend held truth, those "wicked people "had a most lovely memorial in that jewel of a lake.

Gradually the boats were spreading out in a line just clear of the reeds. Scattered black dots began swimming out towards the middle, each leaving its wake as a silver thread in the reflection of the hills. Several flew, legs trailing; scattering the picture on the surface. Coots, coots and more coots—coots everywhere. No, not quite; away over against the rushes was a party of black-and-white birds bobbing about like corks—they at least weren't coots; and through the reeds a procession of swans came weaving—ten, fifteen, twenty, twenty-seven of them made their way out into the lake, where they sat disdainfully admiring their reflections in the water. But still coots came as the boats advanced; scuttering or swimming out towards the middle according to the proximity of their disturber, for I noticed that they liked whenever possible a full two hundred yards between them and the nearest boat.

Then a fusillade—four shots—six—eight—crashed out from the end of the line; two of the boats had jumped a mallard sitting in the reeds. Then suddenly the air was simply full of birds. The black-and-white bunch resolved itself into a party of tufted, wings working furiously to lift their squat bottle-shaped bodies. They rose in a jumbled mass, a hundred or more of them, but as they cleared the reeds the jumble miraculously sorted itself into three perfect "Vs" as they swung out and up and round. Two little lots of teal were in the air, and several mallard; widgeon—the wing bars of the drakes flashed startling clear as they wheeled against the mountain side; pochard—five drakes together, with their red heads gleaming; and three lean long cigar-shaped birds, grey, with white flickerings as their wings beat— What the devil?

"Great crested grebe." William said, "Quite a few breed and several winter here."

One or two of the outlying coots got up and flew slowly off towards the far end of the lake, and a moorhen in the rushes screamed in panic.

But all the birds were wise, and nothing looked like coming near the boats; secretly I wondered at the fullness of our cartridge bags. Nevertheless, it was a fascinating sight—all those different ducks silhouetted against the sky, and showing when they dropped below the skyline the different colours of their kind. Instructive, too, those silhouettes. Absurdly light and slender the teal and widgeon showed beside the heavy, short-winged diving ducks, which even made the mallard look slim and racy. Try as I would I could not pick the pochard from the other divers once they were against the sky, till with a rush a hundred or more forged clear overhead, and there they were, all five of them, in the forefront of the wedge. Size only showed them up—or perhaps their heads looked heavier. The surface feeders were easier by far—the widgeons' tapering and slender necks, short in proportion to the teal and mallard, and the pin tails of the drakes; the mallards' size betrayed them, and their larger, rounded wings; and the midget teal, which in perfect unison swerved and swooped and swung up to the skies again for very joy of flight—yes, it was a spectacle worth seeing, even if our cartridge bags stayed full all day.

The boats were in line now, stretched right across the lake at less than hundred-yard intervals. Most of the duck had disappeared; of the divers nearly all had pitched again towards the farther end, and a few teal, mainly singletons, had dropped back into the reeds, but most of the mallard and all the widgeon had cleared right off in search of pastures new; the three grebes, too, had vanished, though I think they simply followed up the river that led into the lake. But coots remained, and the business of the day was due to start. To be honest, I wasn't looking forward to the massacre.

Slowly the outer boats crept forward, till the line assumed a half-moon shape. Then all were off. Coots rose and circled round in front; untidy fliers and seeming oh, so slow after the duck—but superannuated moorhens? No, not by a very long chalk! Up and up, higher and higher they climbed, till fully two-thirds were almost out of shot. And then they started coming back over the boats and fun grew fast and furious. Maddening things—that limp and straggling flight, legs trailing awkwardly, should make for simple killing—but did it? Hell. They were high, of course, higher far than if plain driven, for here the guns were beaters too, and the birds must pass back over them or leave the lake, which they seemed loth to do.

Birds were falling, though, like sacks, to hit the water with a more than satisfying smack; only somehow they didn't seem to be falling very regularly despite the fact that the barrage from end to end of the line was almost continuous for nearly five minutes. My fears of massacre vanished like snow before the sun. Suddenly William cried: "Look, duck!" My gun was empty, so were my pockets. Where the hell were those ensanguined bags? A single black-and-white bird had lost its head in the din and was trying to break back quite reasonably low across the line. William slew him beautifully and he fairly bounced upon the water.

"Back—after him at once." Two or three of our nearest neighbours were already showing signs of turning, but we swung the Alice Emily about and scuttled back. A golden-eye hen was our reward, with olive head and dirty yellow legs—the magpie duck of the fowler and the first I'd ever handled in the flesh. There was no time to gloat though, as coot were already finding the gap in the line as we flung ourselves on the oars to close it. Time enough to collect mere coot on our return, but "ducks is ducks" and nowhere more than on a public shoot.

Gradually the first wave of the shooting died. There were still a fair few birds ahead, but the first big flush was over as we straightened up the line and advanced once more. But now the lake was narrower and many broke out over the land rather than face the line of boats. Even so, plenty did, and our gun barrels grew quite warm. Duck, too, we saw—tufted and golden-eye; and about forty pochard, all drakes but three; but they came at fantastic heights and only one more dropped, though nearly all received a salutation. Verily this was no mean party. Soon there were reeds ahead, and only a few coot, sick or wise, that scuttered for their shelter. Several boats drove in after them, and scattered shots rang out, though nothing rose.

Firmly William turned for open water.

"I tried that once. Drowning's more comfortable if you feel that way inclined.

Slowly the line formed up again for the return drive and the pick up. Almost all the live coot had gone down on the lake back where we started from and we reckoned we had twenty-one to pick en route. We were lucky to get six ourselves, but it didn't matter, as all that were dead were gathered, and somebody wanted 'em!

The return drive wasn't so successful, as the lake was wider this end, and so were the gaps between the boats. And quite apart from the height they flew at—not one in three was low enough to kill—their eye for gaps was pretty well unerring.

Superannuated moorhens my foot!

We did get one bit of jam, though. As we were slipping in

towards the landing stage, I suddenly spotted a little bunch of duck quite low above the shore—someone in the reeds had a shot, and they swerved clean over us, climbing as best their tiny wings would take them, clapping on every inch of speed they could. Teal would have made the height, or swung aside in time, but these were tufties, as the grey feet of the three immatures we picked up showed.

Lunch was a fairly protracted affair, and not entirely solid. The local kept a goodly brand of beer, and thither we repaired. Moreover, it was Boxing Day and the company was good. All things considered it was not strange that two hours passed before we re-embarked.

The plan was to repeat the morning's manoeuvre, for there still seemed plenty of coots. This time the Alice Emily took the outside berth next to the reeds on the far side. We were early away from the stage and got there with time to spare, so William nosed the boat in towards the shore. Inside the reed bed there was a vast raft of fallen rushes rotting ia the water and as we emerged a dozen snipe departed from it, creaking and swerving off towards the hills.

A buzzard launched himself from off the top of an old stag-headed oak and leisurely flapped away; but before he'd gone a hundred yards a pair of crows appeared and mobbed him, cawing lustily—so poor buzzy started soaring, round and round, to reach the quiet of the upper air. As we watched, a snipe appeared—a tiny speck, swerving erratically across the sky. We froze; he was coming our way—yes—no—yes. His wings closed and he dropped like a plummet straight at our heads. Swoosh, and he was past and away, zig-zagging up to heaven again at an incredibly rate of knots, and four empty cases were bobbing reproachfully in the water alongside. It was as pretty a bit of flying as you could wish to see.

The afternoon was more or less a repetition of the morning. I don't think there were quite so many coots, but to make up for that, lunch had sapped the restraint of many of the guns, and the barrage, if possible, was even more intense. As William put it: "After lunch here a coot's in fair range up to a hundred yards, and any duck in sight." Looking around I was inclined to agree!

One incident stood out. A single pochard, whether pricked or just plain deafened by the din, hadn't quite attained the requisite altitude when he came back over us. We rather muffed him, both of us, but he came down in a long volplane that hit the water near the reed bed over two hundred yards behind. Damn coots— the drive was nearly over anyway. We fairly heaved on the oars and the lap-lap of the water on the Alice Emily's bows changed to a low continuous gurgle.

William stood up. "There he is. No, it's a coot; pull your right hand. That's him." A red head showed for a moment fifty yards out from the reeds.

But we weren't the only ones who'd spotted him, for out of the reed bed pushed a boat containing the three city visitors. Either their lunch had overcome them or they'd just got tired of rowing and laid up behind the line; any way, here they were, and heading for our duck. He, of course, went down at once—the boat drew nearer—then up he bobbed, just bang between the two!

Three guns rose simultaneously—then a fourth, and with an agitated squeak the three guns lowered hastily, for William was standing, his muzzle squarely covering the opposing boat. The inmates waited not upon the order of their going, but fairly fled back to the shelter of the reeds. Whether they thought they had a madman to consider or whether they realized their offence, the result was satisfactory.

"Whew!" muttered William shamefacedly, "that's the first time I've ever pointed a gun at anyone in my life with intent! But they'd ha' damn nigh blown us out of the water if they'd fired. Where's that bloody duck, anyway?"

Presently we spotted him again, eighty yards away, head low along the surface, paddling madly for the reeds. We headed him, just.

Why is a wounded duck in water so devilishly hard to kill? Time and again that bold red head seemed fairly in the middle of the pattern—but always the torn water stilled with nothing in the centre of the circles. Once or twice he may have dived before the shot was fired—to say he beat the shot charge from the flash I think is nonsense with a modern cartridge.

A duck's head turned away along the water is none so big a

target, and a pellet's splash is larger than that pellet's killing area. Myself, with diving ducks in water, I like to carry a few eights for cripple stopping; here we had none and it cost us nine shells and a deal of luck before we got that pochard in the boat. Indeed, with a ripple on the water to aid his hiding, I do not think we ever should.

By then the tumult and the shouting from the end of the lake had died down to a few scattered shots from the heroes who had braved the reeds, and the sun was drop ping very near the limit of the hills. Just one "drive" back, then "finis".

The end came all too soon, despite the growing protest of my palms and backside. But already, as the boats filed slowly back towards the jetty, there was a decided nip in the air, and the shadows were fast sliding down the hills. These winter days were short.

The bag, when it came to be totted up, was astoundingly meagre for the shells expended. In figures, that is; for the fun we'd had was far beyond all price. Old David seemed very glad of our share of the coots; he'd lots of friends who liked them, so he said. William and I had tried them—as soup—once. Anyway, we'd five ducks of fascinating sorts to look at; barring the pochard, they'd test the kitchen's powers of disguise enough.

William's forecast had been more than justified. I felt sure that I should dream that night—of coot, trailing across the sky, impervious to shot; the snipe that swooped and swung and rose again; the steady drive across the sky of a wing of diving ducks and the sun glint on a pochard's head and neck. It'd surely be a happy dream.

Oh, the "city sports"—yes, they did seem a shade distrait when we last saw them, down by the landing stage. Perhaps they had remembered a date elsewhere.

17

January 6

We missed a white Christmas by a week that year. On Boxing Day it started to freeze and kept it up till late on New Year's Eve when thick cloud gathered to blot out the starlight. The temperature rose ominously. I don't think anyone was surprised when the dark man who had. slipped out to usher the New Year in decently returned with snow spangles a-glitter in his hair, or when they rose next morning to greet a world of white. Over a foot of snow came down before the frost set in again.

Winter had at last made up its mind to have a fling, and nightly the wireless spoke of hill roads still impassable with all high passes blocked. Nightly, too, my thoughts ran on quite a different wavelength, for in a week I should be down with William once again. Snow—geese, geese—snow; to me the two were still entirely complementary, and I did so want to see my first goose crumple,

"Come right on in," hailed William, as I was stamping the snow clods off my boots in the cottage porch six nights later. "Only close that door behind you p.d.q. You've got about the most perishing thing in days you've ever spent in front of you tomorrow, but it's no use trying to get acclimatized at this stage of affairs."

In his little gun-cum-sitting room my host had achieved a very respectable fug; a blazing fire of apple logs from the blown-off branch of a Blenheim that I'd helped to cut up earlier in the year set flickering shadows dancing up and down the walls, while a low-down lamp by William's deep armchair cast a vivid pool of light across his knees. And, luxury of luxuries, there was my supper waiting for me on a little table by the armchair's twin. At least, the skeleton of it; for an earthenware pot that bubbled by the fire was sending up the most delightful meaty smell.

"I meant what I said about tomorrow," William presently remarked, "but at least we won't have to get up before it's light. The morning flight's just not on at the moment. No geese about—" my face must have dropped a foot. "No, not here. You see, first the frost froze all the little spuds rock hard and cemented 'em to the ground; then with snow on top to bury both them and the young wheat inches deep, the poor old pinkfeet were fairly stymied, as there's next to no grass hereabouts. A few fed on the salts for a day or two, and I picked up two and a whitefront, but most of 'em hopped it to a better 'ole at once. The weight of the duck as well—except those crazy widgeon. The more I see of them the less I understand them. They've taken to feeding on the saltings in broad daylight now; at least, they were today. And that's what we'll be trying for tomorrow." Then with a grin he added, "I wonder if you'll recognize the place."

There was a certain amount of justification for that last remark, I decided next morning when we arrived down on the sea wall. The tide, according to the tables, had just begun to ebb, though from the scene before my eyes I should have hesitated long before I made a statement. The sea was a restless dull grey sheet that nuzzled into an endless jagged reef of dirty white; within the reef, a frosted grey-green carpet, irregularly streaked with white, spread right up to my feet. There was no wind to speak of, but the air was filled with a ceaseless rustling and scratching as a myriad feather-edged ice-sheets jockeyed one another for position on the falling waters; or a creek-canopy of ice, stretched taut from brim to brim, fell of its own weight as the supporting water left it.

The reef was the product of the earlier and bigger tides that had followed the new moon. Full four feet high, and from twenty to forty yards across, it had been gradually built and forced up a little higher by each increasing flow, till finally the highest flood had left it stranded, safe for ten days or more from further interference from the sea. Only its outer edge was still laved daily and so built wider yet. From its inner edge white crooked tentacles reached out across the hoary saltings, where creeks that flowed beneath the reef had come up, frozen, then shed their skin of ice as the sea recalled them; leaving it clinging whitely to their sides. And with each flood the waters had coated it afresh, till now in many places it was nearly a foot in depth; a foot of rotten flaky treacherous ice that gave or not beneath one's weight entirely as the spirit moved it.

Not a bird of any sort was in sight. I'd never seen the saltings so deserted. As the rustle of the ice pack lessened, a silence that was purest desolation settled down.

"It was just the same yesterday," William told me by way of encouragement. "Not a sign or smell of anything moving till the sea was plumb out of sight across the mud. Then the widgeon started coming. All from the same direction down the coast. Low as you please, rising and falling from head height up to twenty feet or so." Then, quickly, "Looks like the first little lot already—too late for us to split till they've gone by—"

I've always maintained that William had eyes for any thing that moved upon those saltings that would have put most hawks to shame. It was fully quarter of a minute before I picked up the line of wee black dots that swung and fell to salting level, rose, bunched and levelled out again, and ever sped towards us. Ten yards away we stamp-crashed through an ice-pan to the safe cover of a four-feet creek—with twenty or thirty widgeon heading to pass quite close to William's left and a single outrider coming straight to me!

A jammy start, a very jammy start. Gloating I hugged myself as my victim came on and on.

"You take first shot, we must have him," William almost hissed in my ear.

Why "must"?

Then, as I rose to take the biggest gift in history, I realized. No widgeon this, but a pintail drake in all his glory! The tail, the dapper chocolate head and thin white stripe and snowy graceful neck, all snapped themselves at once into my brain; a clear-cut picture, caught and held. Which was just as well, for I missed that pintail shamefully and very clean. Don't ask me how or why—I just don't know, and I felt very near to tears. The first wild pintail I had ever seen—

Dimly I heard William shooting.

"Three down," he answered me, and forebore from further comment. My face must have told him of the pintail's fate. "Come and pick up," he added. "One fell hereabouts," flinging his handkerchief down on a tuft of sage. "Circle this—he's dead enough I fancy."

It was a funny looking widgeon that I presently picked up, though. Slender, long necked, long billed; its feathers more mottled and duck-like altogether—Glory be, it was the wife of the boy I'd missed! She must have been flying with the widgeon company, for the other two William gathered up were widgeon right enough. Pintail at least would figure in the game book now, a thought which drew a little of the smart from out my memory.

"Thass wholly a rum 'un," William quoted Harry. "I never spotted her."

He then proceeded to pull from his game bag, and don, a once-white canvas cape affair, complete with sleeves and hood—a guise that almost made him invisible among the mud-soiled ice-cakes, while I tied a white hanky like a mob cap over my hair to give what camouflage it could. Then we separated. I stayed about a hundred yards inside the ice reef on the saltings, while William built himself a sort of igloo of loose ice cakes on the mud about as far beyond.

And there we settled; for the odd part of this daylight flight was that the widgeon weren't coming in or out, but one way only, parallel to the salting edge. They didn't come over thick or fast either; maybe a party every twenty minutes. Just enough to keep your eyes keen every second to pick out first that cluster of tiny dots that bunched and strung and rose and fell again, and changed so wonder fully fast to duck, then widgeon. In range—on you—flaring up—and past! With maybe the odd bird staying to swell one of the little piles before us.

The drakes were talking? Yes, a little; shrill, short excited whistles. Ducks kurring too, a little. But it was odd how the noises sank into insignificance now the birds themselves were visible. By night it had been the calling that stole the curtain every time.

For over two hours birds kept coming. Not all came kindly, naturally; but we were fairly in their line. Most came to me, in point of fact, hurrying along above the saltings just inside the ice-pack; but William was by no means out of the game, though most of his shots were at singletons or pairs. Daylight as it was, I noticed two or three times that odd birds answered to his call, though never a bunch paid heed. Then, gradually their numbers eased. For over an hour not a bird appeared.

Brrh! William had been right last evening. This was a perishing bitter way to spend a day. That pallid sun was the devil of a long way off, and the frosty blue sky held less than a hint of warmth. I wasn't in the least sorry to see him gingerly picking his way across the ice wall in to me.

"Lunch, I think," came his greeting, "I know a pub not a hundred miles away where they mull beer very nicely; and sausages and ham and eggs will go a long way towards filling up an aching void."

They did. Lean ham, cut thick and grilled just to a turn; while the old ale, spiced and mulled, would have put life into an icicle. I find there's nothing like a large lungful of salting air for compelling fair appreciation of one's victuals.

"Two o'clock—getting on for three. Much virtue in knowing one's landlord," William grinned up at me. "All the same, we might as well get cracking and see if any thing's moving for an hour or so before the evening flight. Tide'll be on the turn quite soon as well, which may make something restless."

So out we went once more. The day had grown no warmer and I shivered as if a cold finger had been drawn right down my spine, despite the comforting glow that now was in my tummy.

Back to the same pits for a start. But never another carefree bunch of widgeon came cavorting along the salting edge. Indeed, I only saw a single other one all day—a drake, accompanied by a single mallard drake, that pitched together in a creek quite close to William. Which was their most grave mistake, though neither lived to profit by it. It fairly was a gift from heaven, for William simply rose up from his igloo and strolled a hundred yards on to the top of them. I saw the mallard fall before the shot noise reached me. The first report to my ears coincided with the widgeon's crumpling.

Then, as the sun began to tinge the sky with rose and saffron, the salting gods staged an absolute mannequins' parade of ducks for our especial benefit. There seemed no rhyme or reason to it, for no two lots were heading in the same direction.

A score of shoveller flew in from off the mud, then circled, high, and flew straight out again. Eleven drakes I made out in the bunch, all black and brown and white and beautiful against a sky of powder blue. Then, without any warning, high angling out from back of the sea wall, came seven pochard drakes; black-chested, rufus-headed aerial torpedoes. Especially fast and powerful they looked after the shoveller, their short wings fairly forcing them ahead. Straight over us they came in line abreast, and William gave them the benefit of a three-inch four which never even made them swing.

"Blight, but you don't see them a lot down here—or shoveller either," said William wonderingly. We were sitting together by a crack in the ice floe debating what to do for the evening flight. There was meat for discussion, too, for nothing seemed to be happening according to the rifles today.

And the saltings hadn't finished their benefit display even yet.

Not very high this time, following the line the shoveller had taken, only closer in, a big duck, flying very straight. Dark head, light belly I could see—but I didn't recognize it beyond the fact that it was undoubtedly a duck and therefore very welcome. My safety catch clicked gently forward as I raised my barrels instinctively across my face.

"Steady, don't shoot," said William, gazing raptly at my whilom target, which wasn't more than thirty yards away and swinging out to sea again. Still I couldn't place it. A long torpedo shape, black head, red beak. Then, as it swung, its pale flank caught the light from the setting sun and lit with such a glorious flash of salmon pink as I have never seen before or since—

"Goosander drake," came William's awestruck voice. "Wasn't he simply lovely?"

How much was plumage and how much pink from the sunset it would be hard to say, nor would I cavil over such a point. We had been afforded such a glimpse of beauty as is not vouchsafed every day.

Still feeling slightly spellbound, we simply spread our selves a quarter of a mile apart along the ice reef to await the evening flight—if any. Never, unless you've a darned good reason, wait within range of one another on the saltings, was one of William's maxims. Space is the one thing there's plenty of, and you never know, you may just spoil the other fellow's only shot.

We shouldn't have done that night, though, for neither of us fired one. Not a duck of any sort came in. Not even a redshank or a curlew moved within our ken, and as the sun went down the cold descended like with the closing of an ice-house door.

It was a raw and chilling cold, moreover. The sunset had faded quickly into a dull grey haze which was slowly thickening into cloud. Never a bird was moving, and it was very nearly dark.

Wait—what on earth was that?

'Way out across the mud, etched black against the very last of daylight, was a silhouette I surely knew! That down-pressed beak, those long and slightly owlish wings that had so often fooled me at the covert side? A woodcock here and now? Silent and forlorn, a very ghost in that scene of bitter desolation, he flitted into darkness and was gone.

But William, to my relief, had seen him too.

"Poor devil, he must be clemmed to come down here," he said. "I haven't seen above one other here before. It's been a day of miracles all round. Just think of it, my Rory —widgeon apart, and they were fun enough for anyone. Lord knows—we've seen pintail and pochard and shoveller and goosander and now that woodcock, any one of them worth remarking on, all in a single day, and with a mallard thrown in as a makeweight. It'll be a long time before you see a day like this again, I reckon."

"You never know; we've tomorrow to come down again," I answered him. Which was exactly where I erred, and the little gods that rule the weather overheard, and chuckled to themselves.

Before we were halfway home the snowstorm was upon us; thick, blinding, muffling, freezing on the screen and headlamps. The last six miles took just above an hour, and William's not an over-cautious driver. Those fen roads have no hedges, but deep dykes alongside.

But I'd no cause for just complaint. My one day, picked at random. The saltings indeed had done me proud.

Twelve widgeon, and a mallard and a pintail.

'What's hit is history,' they say. But I've memory pictures of that day as well that look like living down mere history.

18

January 27

My next long week-end was due on the twentieth, but, as someone once most sapiently remarked, the best laid plans so often come unstuck. William was called away and I was left lamenting. However, by the grace of Allah things were fairly slack in the office at that time, and my uncle agreed to my taking the week-end of the twenty-seventh in its place.

Meanwhile the moon waxed and the frost continued—with my prayers. I imagine the small barometer in my flat could never before in all its life have been tapped so often or so anxiously in so short a space of time.

It was almost light as day as I made my way across the park back to my flat on Thursday night. Full moon in three nights' time, I reflected, though the tiny sliver now missing from her right-hand side seemed not to dim her brilliance in the least. Beneath my feet the ground rang hard as iron, for the month-long frost still held the earth. Most of the snow had vanished in that mysterious way that snow does vanish, even in a frost. Only in the lee of shrubberies and buildings traces still lingered; by day a soiled reminder of the purity that of late had covered everything, but now transfigured by the moonlight's frosted magic into fit carpets for the snow sprites them selves to dance upon.

Lord, but the night was cold. Athwart the beam of a street lamp a host of tiny tinsel flakes came tumbling, all a-glitter as they fell. Maybe a pigeon, roosting coldly up above, had changed from foot to foot, drawing the numbed one that had held its weight back into the soft warmth of its breast feathers.

Glad I was to reach my flat. Another night, and I'd be off to William's, for fondly I was taking his silence to give assent. And then I saw his letter on the table—

"You can take this as a warning," he had written. "From the coastal shooting point of view it's simply not worth coming. The frost's gone on too long, and everything has fled before it. Your bed's still here, and so am I, both very ready to receive you, and the 'snipe pit' still holds a faithful snipe or two. But otherwise the place is verra, verra bare. So you have been warned."

Hells bells and all damnation! Here was another sweet belief gone west. From almost every book and article I'd ever read on fowling I'd gathered that real hard weather was the be-all and end-all of a coastal gunner's prayer; and Lord knows, this was hard enough. Yet here was William saying … I gave it up.

However, my week-ends had come to mean rather more to me than William evidently suspected, and at least he hadn't said "don't come!" So Friday evening found me—following a wire most shamelessly timed to precede my arrival by a bare two hours—once again on William's mat, listening to a cheerful hail bidding me to come in and shut that something door, while Bill's tail thumped a tattoo of welcome on the wall inside.

"Glad I didn't scare you off," said William. "You'll find a spot of supper in the usual place "—nodding towards the brown earthenware pot sizzling by the fireside "and you can have it in comfort in an armchair by the Ike tonight—Mrs. T's out," he added with a grin.

Coast or no coast, I felt that life was not entirely with out its little consolations.

"Sorry I was rather damping in my letter," William went on, "but I'd just got back from one of the blankest early morning flights I've ever seen—my third blank in succession, incidentally—and possibly I was feeling a shade jaundiced in my outlook. There just was nothing there. Not a sign or sound or smell of a bird of any sort, barring a stray pipit or two."

I put the question that had been hovering on my lips for the last two days.

"But surely hard weather's the one thing you're supposed to pray for? In books at least—"

William stared into the fire for quite a while before replying.

"Quick changes rather, I'd say; and hard weather, really hard, anywhere but where you are. Quick changes mean altered feeding, like as not; or altered times of getting there. Frost, flood, fog or snow—they all tend to upset the settled routine that the fowl have got into, and which they know is safe, and force them into new and untried ways. Then, if you're quick in the uptake and also very lucky, is your chance of out-guessing them.

"That's what the weather does. Frost at first seals up the inland feeding and forces stuff down to the coast which doesn't freeze so easily, and where some may wander about in search of food for a few days. But if they find none the weight'll clear off pretty quickly unless the thaw comes.

"That's what's happened here. The geese went first when the wheat and spuds they were feeding on got frozen and then snowed under. A lot of the mallard too. Odd lots of birds appeared that had been driven off from other spots—witness our daytime widgeon— but they soon pass if there's no food to hold 'em.

"All the same, you never can be certain at this game. We cover such a very tiny sector of the coast in our manoeuvrings that we always might be lucky. A little shift of temperature in some obscure corner of the Baltic, or an over eager punt gunner on a Scottish estuary might just serve to fill our corner up overnight and give you and I the flight of our lives at untried fowl! So you've always that thought to take to bed and dream on by way of consolation!"

Consolation indeed! About the last thing I needed under the present circumstances. Two whole days free from any thought of office work or city hours; two days to wander free with the best of friends, a dog and a gun. What did it really matter if the gun grew hot or no? The recipe for happiness was there, accentuated by a spell of London's winter.

Besides, there was always what William called his "snipe pit"— surely an unique addition to almost any small rough shoot. A rectangle of bright green grass perhaps 100 by 150 yards that was almost in the village. One end, in fact, was bounded by the village street, while no fewer than seven cottages, as well as the buildings of a sixty-acre holding, backed on to its two long sides. The fourth side, which alone was free, abutted on to neighbour ing territory and so was out of bounds.

Now in the heart of this very ordinary seeming little field was a very slight depression where the grass, come rain or snow or frost or shine, stayed always the most vivid emerald. And therein lay the secret. For the effluent of all the drains of all the seven cottages—publish it not in County Council circles—as well as the surplus liquid from the holding midden—which last, as William pointed out, was shocking waste of good manurial value—seeped down by sundry channels to the sump hole in the middle.

There, curiously enough, a clear little spring bubbled up to mingle with, dilute and spread the richness which came drifting down into its orbit. There was no outlet to the field, but ten feet from that spring, all round, the ground was firm and hard. Yet that small patch was always soft to probing bills and of a richness quite extraordinary.

Now worms like soft rich ground; and snipe like worms. The connection here is obvious.

All through the winter the snipe pit was a safe bet for a bird or two, but with the onset of cold weather it might hold anything. One day William had counted no fewer than forty-three from the road, on his way back from Church! Up to a score was in no way unusual.

But how to deal with them most effectively? That was the burning question. Walking them up was hopeless. Accustomed to human beings round the cottages and farm as they must have been, let so much as an alien whisker cross the deadline of the hedge that marked the field and hey presto! a young grenade burst from around the pit, snipe flinders whisking wildly everywhere. Driving was the usual method we adopted, which had the advantage that we could count on doing it twice the same day, for some snipe nearly always had returned by the afternoon. Not quite the same drive, of course, unless the wind or weather forced us. They learnt, those birds.

But William had another and far more deadly way of coping

with them. True it necessitated an east wind to put into practice, a state of affairs, which, when you want it, is none too common.

The game was to cast your bread upon the waters by putting the snipe away quite quietly and un-shot-at, which required, I maintain, great moral courage! Then simply to kneel upon the grass a few yards upwind of the "pit". Hence the east wind, for the only houseless hedge was at the west end of the field, and we found that any snipe returning in to pitch would always head the wind, from whatever point it blew; and not even the most long- suffering cottager likes to have his dwelling sprinkled promiscuous-like with No. 8. It seems to make him nervous.

After putting the snipe away quietly, it was surprising how soon the first of them returned. Ten minutes at most, and you'd see or hear from a tiny speck zig-zagging around quite leisurely among the clouds. A circuit or two, high up—they never seemed to mind the new animals grazing their field provided no large pink faces were raised enquiringly to the heavens—then wings would fold close into pencilled flanks, and swoosh I in one long, dizzy, hurtling dive the snipe was there. Wings open just above ground level, flatten, check, and—well, the rest was really up to you. It was an intriguing form of shooting; daytime flighting almost. Seven in just about as many minutes was William's solo record and with two of you the opportunities of an eye wipe lent added zest.

Today, alas, the wind was wrong. We were to try a drive. It was rather a particular drive, though, for William and I secreted ourselves in the gardens of the three cottages which flanked the north side of the field. And these three cottages belonged to three very remarkable old ladies—the three R's, William called them— Mesdames Rothery, Rye and Rudd, who each lived quite alone. None of them minded the temporary usurpation of their gardens in the least; in fact, I think they all felt a little flattered; but their individual reactions rather varied, to say the least. Mrs. Rothery, who occupied the centre cottage, would, as soon as William had spoken to her, dive straight away into her doorway. Bang! Clatter! Smack! and every window sash came rattling down and every curtain pulled together. Then, her fortifying done, Mrs. Rothery herself would peer, witch-like, from between the puce horrors of the parlour, which failed to meet across the window by a full three inches; and there she stayed till all the tumult and the shooting died away. An interesting performance; I often wondered what she thought its object was. Nevertheless, she was always genuinely annoyed to miss a "shoot"!

Mrs. Rudd was fat and beaming, garrulous almost beyond belief. From the moment you entered the orbit of her garden to that when you disappeared over her far horizon, a steady stream—spate almost—of ailments past, present, and to come, sluiced warmly down on your defenceless head. Snipe and their movements held for her no faintest interest. Here was a god-given victim, actually standing in her garden, and the vials of her speech were emptied copiously.

Not so Mrs. Rye. Her late lamented had been a gamekeeper, and must have trained her well, for she took a really keen interest in what was toward. She always stood beside and just behind you, never chattered, and her rare remarks were quiet and to the point; moreover she could mark. O si sic omnes!

Today, alas, I'd drawn the outside "butt". Upon me had the lot of Mrs. Rudd fallen. Sure enough, as soon as I hove in sight, out the old dear paddled, and straightway started off nineteen to the dozen in a voice to wake the dead. But mercifully she was soon cut short—before she'd even told me what the doctor found when he cut her husband open.

"Look up—over!" Harry's stentorian bellow came as a reprieve.

A whirr—a cheerful little creak—Whirr! Whirr! all round and over me. Partridges; seven—eight—nine of 'em. They must have been picking round the holding stack yard where the clover hay was piled. One little cock came straight between the cottage chimneys, not twenty feet above me. Against the pallor of the frost-reflecting sky, each detail stood out clear. His russet throat and forehead, the small, pink-wattled diamond round his eye, and soft grey pencilling that split about a grand rich horseshoe and shaded into white below his ruddy undertail and clear clean underwing. He was as complete a little picture as the eye could wish to see.

Almost was I tempted—almost; he gave me such a perfect chance. But William holds most strongly—and indeed in my more sober moments, so do I—that any partridge on a harried small-time shoot that reaches Christmas Day unscathed has earned the freedom of his countryside. So my little cock-bird's panic swerve on seeing me was labour wasted, and he reached his peak and, set-winged, singled in to join the covey in their gentle glide towards the frost-bound earth.

So much I saw, and so much only. Mrs. Rudd had not even time to get fairly launched into the tale of the awful fate that had overcome the twins, before they were up—

Scaipe, scaipe—a dozen elfin pencil scrapings half-muffled by the buildings. The partridges had given them a lead, moreover, and right nobly did they follow it. Straight in between the chimneys, plumb in my little cock-bird's passage, came one snipe, and fluffed and tumbled as I turned and swung on him. Another, flicking low between the cottages, zoomed upwards at sight of me, hanging clear for a second against the sky. Then he too tumbled, and I had achieved a right and left. It didn't often happen so.

William had picked another, so the pit had done us well.

Our next port of call was the Wilderness, that wide, shallow, bracken- and broom-filled quarry where I'd last been in September after partridges.

"Don't shoot a hen," William said. "But there's at least two ancient warriors I hear going up to roost most evenings, and we might catch one of 'em on the wrong foot. I'm hoping we may find the odd bun lying rough, 'cos Harry and I spent the best part of Thursday afternoon trying to upset their domestic arrangements by shoving bits of newspaper dipped in an evil-smelling compound of tar and paraffin down their holes. With this dry weather some of ' em may have taken the hint."

I thought of the head-high waste we'd ploughed through in September, and rather fancied that even if they had, the odds might lie rather heavily with our quarry!

However it was a very different seeming Wilderness that I looked down on to five minutes later. William had given me a roving commission along the rim of the quarry, with instructions to keep a few yards ahead of Harry and he and Bill, as they crashed through down below; and from where I was, I got a wonderful bird's-eye-view of the whole scene.

The snow of three weeks past, checked in its sweep across

the open fields by the sudden dip, must have drifted deep over the quarry floor, for it still weighed bracken and brambles down beneath a solid crust. Only the gorse and broom and blackthorn clumps thrust darkly through. The rest was plain white hummocks, crossed and criss-crossed with a maze of tracks made before the surface snow had crispened; tracks which emerged mysteriously from one white hummock to vanish just as cleanly in another.

The ensuing hour was decidedly entertaining, and must have benefited the cartridge manufacturers not a little. For the stinking out had worked to admiration, and the ground was fairly stiff with rabbits lying rough. The snag was that they were quite invisible beneath the snow. There was no warning of their movement, no tell-tale twitching bracken frond to focus the attention. Simply an elongated furry form, dark in shadow, pale in the sunlight, that catapulted itself with incredible velocity out of one snowed up hummock into another precisely similar—and there was no outward means of telling whether that second snow cap lay over a bramble clump or solid earth. It was all most disconcerting, and speed, speed, speed, was the essence of the game. Second barrels were almost at a discount; there was little enough time even for second thoughts. And that was very nearly my undoing.

A flick of brown in the rabbit run that led out from a snow hill, and I almost overbalanced in a frantic last split-second effort not to take the trigger up that final hair's breadth. For the brown most unfairly had developed wings and after a preliminary hop and skip, a perfectly good hen pheasant whirred away.

I glanced across at William. He was gazing after the departing bird. Harry stared straight in front of him, perhaps a thought too raptly to assuage a slightly guilty conscience.

All the same, it was a useful warning. In quick succession, five more hens burst forth. Never a sign of their long-legged consort, but William at least was beaming happily.

Meanwhile the hound Bill was having the time of his young life, diving from drift to drift, disappearing completely while the snow crust heaved and cracked above him. Wild outbursts of enthusiasm marked the discovery of yet another bun; a discovery shortly followed by the upthrust of an eager snow-splashed face trying to find out if those wretched guns had let him down again or not.

Yes, it was beyond all question a crowded hour. By the time we reached the far end of the pit Harry's stick was getting pretty crowded with its furry burden.

Right in the farthest corner I caught a tiny mouse-movement almost beneath my feet, where the side curled vertical and overhung a little. A glimpse of an apoplectic red-cheeked face and smoky tawny eye, and the master of the harem launched himself in all his glory.

Now it may have been pure chance—I'd hate to say it wasn't— but that cock pheasant chose to fly low and straight at Harry, then on to pass not six feet over William, and William at that particular moment was deep in a tangled thicket of broom and gorse that reached to well above his head. Not a shot was fired, and in a silence too deep for mere words, I watched the old filibuster sail right out and over the village clear to the fen beyond—lower and lower, till suddenly his head and wings flung back and tail fanned open, waggled a moment as the wind checked through it—and he was down. He ran a few steps to collect his balance, drew himself up a-tiptoe in his pride, shook himself, then walked away sedately down a dyke as if he had no care in all the world. I laughed. I simply couldn't help it. Forced out into the open, and with every thing against him, he'd still defeated us so very handsomely.

Ten minutes later the situation was reversed. We were on the return beat, all three of us ploughing through patches of head-high broom and bracken and brambles just tall enough to spill the snow they carried well down inside my gumboots.

William called over to me," Keep your eye on Bill, Rory, he's working up to something."

Keep an eye on Bill! Rather a counsel of perfection under the circumstances. At the moment he was in a comparatively open space just ahead of me, nose down, questing in little short rushes, missing the line and casting himself, tail going nineteen to the dozen.

"Pheasant for a ducat! Likely that other old cock." William was drawing in towards me.

Then Bill was off. Straight to the side of the quarry and scrambling up its face by a rabbit track that looked as if it might have offered foothold to a fly. Over the crest, and out of sight.

His master's piercing whistles had, alas, not the least effect, and I caught a look on William's face that boded no good toward the errant hound whatever.

Then I was pounding off back at my best pace towards a spot a hundred yards away where the quarry wall had crumbled.

Vain hope. Before I'd got half-way, I heard the clatter of wings and a derisive chuckle from well beyond the sky line. Pest on him! Sadly I started to retrace my steps.

But the old warrior this time had made a very grave miscalculation. Maybe he thought we'd left the pit, or maybe he just didn't think at all and only remembered all those attractive girls he'd left in such dangerous proximity to their other boy friend. Be that as it may, back he came sailing over the quarry's edge plumb between William and myself.

Just grand he looked in the gleam of the frosty sunlight. As he did his best to bank and climb above us it stroked his flank into a glory of golden bronze, black tippeted. So for a second—

I don't know which of us slew him, but there was no doubt whatsoever who took to himself all credit for the whole affair. I've seldom seen a dog look so insufferably conceited as Bill did when he produced the victim from among the brambles where it had fallen and delivered it up to his master. He was grinning from ear to ear. And William, as he took the offering, broke into a reluctant grin himself.

"Some tripehounds are born lucky," he said gruffly, rubbing his hand affectionately over the old dog's head.

We didn't waste too much time over lunch. January days aren't overlong at best, and we hadn't really made our minds up whether to try a flight that evening or not. Meanwhile there was quite an acreage of fen to cover, though William pointed out that the sum total of our efforts there was likely to prove of more use as an aid to digestion than an increment to the larder. Harry would join us later, after sorting out the foxes' feed.

Crisp, hard and crackling the fen was, and bone-dry everywhere. Even the dykes were whitely shining skims of ice with water maybe several inches down below. Bill worked the rushes manfully, but nowhere did we find a sign of life, save when a blackbird, still searching hopefully for any crumbs left over from the hawthorn feast two months ago, fled screaming down a hedgerow.

"See there—" William nodded towards a couple of fresh-flung molehills where the soil showed black and new, "I've heard tell that when they come up to work again after a spell of cold, the thaw's not far behind."

I glanced up at the chill blue sky. It didn't look to me as if it would ever thaw again, and there wasn't a cloud in sight. But—something else was. I saw him first, moreover, which pleased me not a little! Three fields away—an old cock pheasant skulking down a dykeside towards a scrubby fence that led back to the road. Head low, and every feather pressed tight in; he didn't know we'd seen him, for he merged most wonderfully with the frosted greens and browns around him.

"He wins," William said quietly, "road's my boundary and he hasn't sixty yards to go. No, by Jove, he doesn't—yet! There's Harry, and I'll bet he's come down on his bike."

William was off full tilt. I tumbled to his plan and carried quietly on as if nothing was toward. William met Harry, rushed on to the road and retrieved the bicycle from the dyke wherein it lay. Slipping the shells out from his gun he went creaking rapidly way up the road. His method of carrying the weapon struck me as quite ingenious, for he had quickly shrugged out one sleeve of his coat, stuck the stock in one game pocket, and put the coat on again, so that the barrels stuck up behind his neck. It needed a straight back, but the gun was safe and firm enough.

Almost he made it—almost. He was skidding wildly to a standstill, both feet flat down on the road—the only means of braking Harry's bike possessed—when the old cock, just as if he knew full well what all the fuss was over, nipped out from the hedge and calmly ran—ran, mark you, straight across the road and on to alien territory. The sight was altogether too much for Bill, who plunged wildly forward. But the cock was safely out of court and William only leaned across the handlebars and watched him go.

"Wonder if it's our old friend of this morning," he said as I came up. "If it is, he'll have a tale to tell his wives tonight."

It might have been. At any rate it was the only one we saw that afternoon.

Two coveys of partridges were feeding down among the rushes.

Although the cold weather had caused them still to hang together as a family, it was noticeable when they flew that the coveys seemed made up of pairs rather than single birds. A few minutes later. Bill almost caught a singleton which flew rather lazily across our front. And William, without a moment's hesitation, shot it. I was inclined to be facetious till I saw the emaciated scrap of skin and bones he carried. The feathers below its tail were foul and draggled, and the whole bird couldn't have weighed above eight ounces. Carefully William enlarged a mole run and stamped the body in to bury it.

"He'd have died within a week if I hadn't shot him," he said. "I'm always losing birds with this filthy disease down on the fen. Mostly a bit later on than this. I reckon it's because it's always damp enough to give the worms that cause it every chance. And all 1 can do is to shoot and burn or bury any bird that I see has it badly. It's a sad fact that you find devilish few healthy coveys reared down here."

This was the only chance the fen produced, though we could have slain a hare. But there was still the snipe pit to do.

This time I was in Mrs. Rye's front garden and out she came to watch, saying she's heard how well I'd shot this morning, and only wished she'd stood with me to see it! History, alas, did not repeat itself. The only snipe that came I missed with much completeness, to have my eye wiped simply beautifully by William from the next-door garden. He must have put a pellet in its head, for that snipe spun stiff-winged like a paper windmill to the ground. So Mrs. Rye was satisfied, though I fear my reputation in that quarter was not much enhanced.

By now it was three o'clock. To flight or not to flight, that was the question of the moment. I must say I was all in favour; but then I hadn't visited the coast for a fortnight, and my last trip there had been very far from barren. Gently I reminded William that it had been he who pointed out those molehills only an hour ago!

"Right. On your own head be it," was the reply, "but I'm betting you the drinks at Mother Goss's on the way back that we come home 'clean'."

It is on record that William bought those drinks. For all that, I don't think his judgment was so much to blame.

We found most perfect cover in among the ice-floes, but not a single duck or widgeon came in off the sea, and never a curlew called. Even the restless redshanks were conspicuous mainly by their absence, and only the gulls came drifting ghostly quiet from off the land at sunset. Poor devils, the Lord knows what they found to eat this weather.

I saved my money by picking up a mallard—and what a mallard! A razor-breasted, salting scavenger too sick or lazy to follow up his fellows when they left in search of fresher pastures, he dropped into a creek two hundred yards away and let me walk him up against the orange afterglow.

We didn't wait for moonrise. The sky was pricked with a million points of stars, and never a bird was moving.

It didn't seem worthwhile, even to me. Besides, my ill-gotten drink was clamouring for collection.

19

JANUARY 28

Next evening over supper, apropos of nothing in particular, William suddenly remarked: "I've had a restless sort of want-to-do-something-but-don't-know-what feeling on me all day today. Shall we go and have a look at the coast when the moon gets up? It'll be a lovely evening for a walk down there and we've tons of time to give you a spot of shut-eye before your train."

It struck me as a good idea. Oddly enough, I'd had that restless feeling too. Heaven alone knows why, since we'd had a pretty busy day. In the morning we'd walked miles, each with a bag of tailings over our shoulder, scattering a handful here and there in chosen places. In the lee of a straw stack, close against some broom, or in sheltered spots along the sunny side of a hedge where partridges in warmer days had held their dust-baths. Odd bramblings and chaffinches and other more or less welcome creatures would doubtless share the feast, but the partridges should benefit as well.

"It's all right now the season's as good as finished," William had said, "but I don't like doing it earlier on a shoot of this size. It's apt to put funny ideas into neighbours' heads over boundary pheasants, which is a state of affairs to be avoided at almost any cost."

In addition to our morning's activities, moreover, we had spent the afternoon most heartily, widening with slashers a ride beside the rabbit warren with an eye to improving the summer rifle shooting. Yet still that restless feeling had persisted. It felt almost as though a thunderstorm was pending, which as Euclid well might have put it, was absurd.

So ten o'clock saw William and I rather sheepishly slipping our guns into the car on either side of a most delighted Bill. He, at any rate, viewed the present situation with unqualified approval.

"Oh, I shan't take more than a belt," William replied to my query over cartridges. In truth, even that seemed excessive on the last night's form.

I'd borrowed one of William's white overall affairs. These were short slip-over jackets, complete with hood, made out of stout twill after the pattern of a type of Eskimo garment. No pockets, no buttons, but straps to fasten the wrists. Camouflage was their main object, William had said, but I found it pretty hot walking across the saltings wearing mine, so took it off and stuffed it in my game bag.

Or was it entirely William's garment that was responsible for my moistened brow? It struck me, when presently we paused for a breather, that there wasn't quite the sting in the night air there had been of late. Nor had the stars quite got that diamond hardness in their glitter.

Then William was listening tensely, head on one side, lips slightly parted, and in a moment, I'd heard it too. How right he'd been when first he'd told me of widgeon calling underneath the moon! There's a thrilling urgency about it that will always set my heart a-quiver like no other sound there is. Even the glorious clamour of a goose-skein must take second place—for me. And here, across the starved and frozen saltings, came a goodly company, to judge by the joyous talk they held among themselves. In a moment we could hear wings too, their tempo rising, rising; but out of sight they passed, and gradually the cheerful concourse faded.

But its magic hadn't. Their passing might have been the kiss that woke the sleeping beauty, for almost in a flash it was apparent that the frozen spell of death in life had left the saltings.

Wings there were; wings everywhere. Big wings that whistled, and little wings that shrilled in passing. Beyond all guessing now the moon and stars had dimmed their glitter. Many had vanished altogether, and the cut-ice brilliance of the moonlit saltings was slowly softening and becoming more mysterious. The life that had fled was now returning, heaven alone knew whence.

William and I split up a little, kneeling a hundred yards or so apart on either side of a short-grass patch that was just about in the middle of the saltings. And over us and round us both came widgeon. We didn't see so many, but we heard a lot, and all we heard were on the move in no particular direction. And—we'd only brought a belt of shells apiece. That was the brutal truth. Even an old campaigner like William had been squarely caught. Safe in my ignorance I couldn't help but chuckle just a little.

In point of fact, I don't think we should have slain much more if we'd had a bag full each, for the very reason that the birds were moving nowhere in particular, but simply junketing around the saltings so that it was pure chance if they came over us in sight or not. The sky was poor, as well; low misty cloud that was formless and gave little background despite the moon's best efforts. It was a night that bore out fully William's dictum that ears, not eyes, are the night flighter's greatest asset. I found that by keeping my head down till the noise of wings seemed very close indeed I'd not only a better idea from what direction the birds were coming, but also my eyes were free from strain and likelier by far to pick them up at once. Probably the score or so of shells that I loosed off were all I should have fired in any case. But I missed the confidence that an ample store begets. Birds for a change were plentiful —we might so well have missed our opportunity through purest laziness.

It was the thought of my cursed train that forced us finally to move. The earlier mistiness had ripened into rain, and in all directions we could hear widgeon talking happily. Less urgency about their calling, now, though. The bustling wing sibilant chorus was far less common, and in its stead came the long clear stationary whistling of a cock bird on the ground. A cock bird calling down the clans to dine; for the thaw was here in earnest, and the ban of starvation had been lifted from the saltings. It was with a light heart that I travelled back to town that morning, for I had been privileged to be present at a miracle.

20

February 5

Five days only, and here I was bound William-wards once more. The rain, which was spangling the outside of my carriage window as I travelled down, had continued pretty well non-stop since last Sunday evening. Nevertheless, as I neared my journey's end, the train grew more and more crowded. Each halt produced its quota of embarking passengers, mainly younger folk, till by the time we reached William's nearest market town both corridors and compartments were cram-jammed full.

"'Tis the fair, for sure." A cheerful looking youngster answered my query, and went on to explain how every year about this time booths and merry-go-rounds appeared from all directions heading for the market place in the centre of the town; how they filled it entirely to the grave dislocation of the local traffic; and how for a whole week folk from the villages around came there a-fairing.

"Always it has been held so. Nor they couldn't change it without an Act of Parlyment. Much as some might like," my informant added darkly.

As we drew in the station lamps cut gleaming paths over the wet paving of the platform and raindrops flickered steadily through the beams. A gust of wind brought the blare of a distant merry-go-round and 'way over the town I could see the naphtha flares reflected from low-hanging clouds. As the congestion aboard eased, I mentally thanked my stars that my pursuit of pleasure did not lead me fairing on such a night. Then chuckled as a thought struck me; but no, the moon was down by now—William would hardly take me mud-larking tonight!

Next morning, when I looked out of my bedroom window, the fen below appeared as a series of rather spotted steel grey mirrors held in by thin green frames. After the sudden thaw and the rain that had fallen steadily ever since, the floods were well and truly out, and almost the only land that showed over the whole expanse were the narrow strips of built-up dykes and driftways.

"That pretty well rules them out as a source of your week-end's amusement," said my host. "No snipe—they'll not stand above a little wet—and though I've been watching pretty closely, the duck seem to have disappeared. There were a few widgeon there along toward the middle of the week—yes, day-time as well—but the water's got too deep for 'em to feed and they've hopped it.

"Likely there may be some feeding on the saltings o'nights 'cos these floods must have upset quite a bit of their inland feeding arrangements. Once the water floods more than an inch or two above the grass roots widgeons begin thinking of fresh pastures.

"Not much help from the moon unless we get something pretty special in the way of skies, and that don't look too likely." Glancing out of the window. "Still and all, we might go and prospect, if only this ruddy rain would ease up a bit."

The weather, however, declined to co-operate. A steady silent soak fell from dull unbroken clouds, and there wasn't a breath of wind to shift the pall.

All morning we watched it tracing down the window, stirring the muddy ground outside; trying to persuade our selves that no highly problematical widgeon was worth the chill discomfort of a very damp and clammy shirt, and becoming more and more depressed in the process. By lunch time we had pretty well reasoned ourselves into a fine fit of the sulks.

"To hell with it," William burst out as we finished the meal, "a drop of rain won't kill us."

Reason or no, sulks vanished as we stepped outside and a ridiculous feeling of conscious virtue took their place; while Bill quite clearly showed his sentiments with the whole weight of his latter end.

Since the main object of the exercise was to try to discover if and where any widgeon had been feeding, we headed towards the north shore first, for along the four miles stretch of salting here were scattered half a dozen patches of short green grass, any of which, provided it was wet enough, widgeon were apt to visit. These patches dried or flooded according to the recent tides and weather; and today, with six days and nights of continuous rain as well as the biggish tides that had followed the new moon, we thought they should be very nicely awash.

Thus far we'd got in our plannings and prophecies when William swung the old car off the main road and on to the last lap of the journey—a mile and a half stretch of rutted lane that led down to the sea wall.

Lane—hell! A muddy canal stretched out before us, all pocked with falling raindrops. The old bus coughed to a standstill.

"Here's where we walk," said William. "The sea wall isn't more than half a mile across those fields, and I know old Jakes who farms them pretty well. That is, unless you'd rather go home?" with the lift of an eyebrow in my direction.

My reply was short, but I flatter myself not entirely unintelligible.

That half mile was one of the most murderous I've ever covered. Black gumbo, rain sodden and deep ploughed right to the dyke edge. Thigh boots were not the ideal footwear, and both of us were pretty hot and sticky as we ducked beneath a single strand of wire and clambered up the slope of the sea wall, with Bill a short ten feet ahead.

As he topped it—Aank—a split second's silence as we froze in utter disbelief, then the wild clamour of a hundred throats as a fair sized gaggle of pinks who had been feeding on the saltings quite close in, took off and became a dwindling skein.

"Down, damn you, down," came William's agonized insistence as Bill trotted back to see what we were playing at. I was already on my face, with an empty feeling where my lunch should be and my heart going in great lurching jumps.

Another chance—so near and yet so far. Those geese had been feeding or resting on one of the very patches of that close clipped grass we'd come down to investigate for signs of widgeon. A patch within a hundred yards of where we lay. Actually I doubt if they'd have been approachable in any case, but that balm had not had time to sink in yet.

It was curious hearing the sounds we'd so often heard from the other end. The single note, the mad clamour as the geese had jumped, the period of silence as they took up flight positions and finally the steady chorus—only now it was diminishing, not swelling.

Interesting, too, to see how quickly the jumping rabble sorted itself. Already, and long before they'd reached the salting edge four hundred yards away, they'd formed two long slim lines abreast; two strings of evenly spaced beads, the one a shade above the other. Then, as we watched, the upper string foreshortened and came together; clotted and then drew slowly out again—

"Blast—will you look at them!" a furious and quite unnecessary whisper at my side. "Slip along there fifty yards or so. They've gone completely crazy."

I waited not upon the order of my going. Back down the sea wall—a frantic stumble through the clutching tufts of marram with my sea boots going clump, clump, clump and fingers scrabbling at my shell belt for those "precautionary "BBs—not wholly daring to believe that what we'd seen could really be quite true.

For the upper of those skeins of geese had swung right round and headed straight back to us. As I breathlessly parted the grasses at the top of the sea wall they still were coming, and not two hundred yards away. Nor were they over high.

Oh, those next few seconds—

Straight on they came, straight on and over both of us. Vast grey shapes, quite unmissable. Yet even so, I missed first barrel— and so did William. I saw his one goose fall in that same never-to-be-forgotten moment as my bird curled his neck. They hit the ground almost together. I fear I ran in most disgracefully. Thigh boots and all, I had Bill beaten from the start.

My first goose lay breast downwards on the short grass; grey wings half open, sepia neck flung sideways. I stooped to pick him up, and turned towards the sea bank feeling rather weak and curiously drained of all emotion.

Bill proudly preceded me; half-dragging, stumbling a little over his outsize burden.

When I flung down beside them, William stayed silent. I guess he knew how I was feeling— Gradually my jumbled thoughts straightened themselves.

Here was my first goose, all undeserved. Slain in broad daylight, without a breath of wind or weather to assist. Walked up like a partridge, practically. And just because of his one mistake he lay there. Those great strong wings—

Then I thought of those other days when the geese had so handsomely defeated us. A fluke had brought this tangible result, but it wasn't the end or even the full object of the chase. That, somehow, was wrapped up in the fuller understanding of the spirit and moods of the ever-changing expanse of sea and salting that surrounded me; and of adventures past, present, and pray God, yet to come.

But—this was my first goose. Today was a definite landmark along that road. And with the thought a rich warm glow of triumph in this, and thankfulness for all those other days, came stealing over me. Still the rain continued steadily. But now I was proofed against mere rain.

"A very pleasant little interlude. I never dreamt we'd see a goose down here so soon after the frost." William sounded almost aggrieved. "We'd best get cracking though. There's quite a walk ahead of us if we're to get round all these flashes."

Our first objective, which was where the geese had been, looked simply perfect. Little pools had flooded out and linked together so that the whole centre of the acre and a half patch of turf was awash; the short grass vying with the raindrops to stipple the surface of the water. A dining room laid out, it would have seemed, to tempt the palate of the most fastidious widgeon.

Slowly we circled it. There was old sign here—a very little; flattened and nearly washed out by the rain. Odd waders—shank, curlew, dunlin, plover—had been here lately as the whitewashed splashes showed; maybe in search of drowned-out insects, or perhaps to drink the brackish water. Odd patches of tiny pink and white shell fragments told of shelduck visitors. "Our" geese— yes; their sign was plain enough. The scattered green and white droppings said that they were grass-fed, too; but these were few and very recent. Where they'd walked through the plashy grass bent stems were still slowly straightening. It was all too clear, theirs had been but the chance visit of an hour and they were not likely to return.

All this we read; but our script said naught of recent widgeon.

There were still four other likely flashes to canvass, though. With this one in such perfect order it seemed more than likely that the others might be too; and as William remarked, those widgeon must be feeding somewhere.

Tide was 'way out, and the salting creeks we jumped or clambered over held only muddy trickles and little scuttling crabs. All the same we managed to collect a fairly representative selection of that mud about our guns and persons. It is a curious fact that rain on the saltings always seems to make their substance so infinitely more pervasive.

We had one little skirmish with some scattered curlew which William tried to drive to me. I went on hah a mile and snuggled in a creek just where the saltings fringed off into mud. When I was settled William started along the mud edge to me, but suddenly dived for cover as an in coming bird looked as if it might give him a chance. It didn't, of course; and presently the ones we were after dribbled past me just comfortably out of range, to pitch a quarter of a mile beyond and unconcernedly resume their feeding.

But when we met again, William and I just stopped and stared, then burst out laughing. Splashed mud had smeared, and the rain had done the rest. William, I think, had pushed his hair back with his hand, forgetting the condition of that hand. Neither of us were in a fit state to be introduced into a drawing room.

I fancy that we were both fairly optimistic over what we should find at one or other of those flashes ahead. After the start we'd had, today was a day that simply couldn't fizzle out; and I know that I at least, possibly on account of the comforting and unaccustomed lump reposing in my pocket, was entirely irrepressible. Which was fortunate. For when we reached the sea wall an hour and a half later we had visited all four flashes; all had seemed to us just perfect— grass awash with brackish water seeping in among the roots—but unaccountably the widgeon did not appear to share our view.

On the way back to the car we decided that if we were to enjoy our sleep tonight, we just must check up on two small possibilities beyond the estuary. At least we'd know then that no weight of widgeon were feeding on "our" ten-mile stretch of saltings.

Although that other side was well in sight, it entailed a half-hour's journey round by road to get down to where we wanted. Lucky it was, a lane led down quite close, as it was four o'clock and drawing in to dusk by the time we reached the sea wall.

"Time's getting on—you'll find a flash out that way." William waved vaguely towards the left. "Can't miss it—it's within a hundred yards of the wall you're on. I'll just check on another little spot and come over your way for the flight. We might get a crack at a mallard—"

We parted. I found my objective easily enough, and it looked as altogether perfect as the other five we'd visited. Slowly I tramped round, peering. Down the far side—yes—yes—widgeon had been here—lately. Here were green and white droppings, exact miniatures of those of the grass-fed geese; and here the grass was torn about, a little. Fresh widgeon, certainly, but not above a very few.

Still, I thought I'd spend my dusk flight here and hope they'd come in early. Indeed, they'd have to if I was to see them; for although the rain was easing, the cloud banked low and solid across the sky, too thick by far to allow a callow five days' moon to help.

From away off down the saltings, came the bump of a single shot, and I looked around to see if Bill had work to do. Bill wasn't visible, but his master was putting on a pretty odd performance. Silhouetted against the mud, he wildly waved his arms, then stopped, with one arm pointing stiffly towards the shore; took a few steps inland, and went through the same queer rigmarole again. Then I tumbled. For some reason best known to himself, William had apparently decided against a flight, and wanted me back at the car.

Rather crossly, I made my slow way back. Perversely the possibilities of the place I left grew rosier as I left it, and I was quite prepared to be a little terse with William.

As I reached the car he straightened up from ferreting behind the seat and solemnly handed me my cartridge bag. And as he spoke his eyes were lit and his voice was fairly quivering with excitement.

"That flash looks like a ruddy farmyard where the widgeon have been feeding. I've seldom seen the likes. With any luck we're going to have some fun, my Rory."

"With this sky?" I answered rather dampingly. "It'll be black as a Hebrew's armpit in an hour."

"I'm—not—so—very—sure. I've a hunch, at least. You see, the town's a bare three miles—in a bee-line."

Nor would the maddening creature vouchsafe any clearer information.

However, the flash he presently led me to showed sufficient evidence to make any fowler's blood run a little faster. Picture a lawn set in an almost boundless foot-thick border of grey-green crabgrass, its centre flooded to a depth of inches only. Along the water's edge on the down-wind side a yard-wide floating scum of oil and bitten grass ends—ends bitten short by widgeon, oil from off their plumage. All round, flat trodden grass with regular runways reaching in among the fresher pasture; the turf all scarified and ragged about by probing beaks and everywhere thick-scattered widgeon droppings, fresh as paint.

"A ruddy farmyard" just about described it. They must have been a goodly company that dined last night.

The whole flash wasn't more than fifty yards across, and the creek that drained it was a bare six inches deep and not a foot across.

"No cover there," said William as we rather gloatingly encircled our discovery.

"Dull and dark as tonight's going to be, it couldn't matter less. We'll be quite invisible squatting on the ground. The only thing I'm not quite happy over is the size of the place. There's been plenty widgeon feeding here—they may take it into their incalculable heads they've skimmed the cream off it. Still, we'll know soon enough."

The flash was too small to make it worth while splitting up so we sat down close together at the east end, in order to have the last of daylight for a backcloth to anything that might drop in.

With dusk the rain left off entirely, and a tiny, very tiny breeze came stroking in from seaward. I hoped it might give the birds a tendency to pitch against it—it's so much easier to cope with one-way traffic in the dark!—but it struck damp and clammy through our sodden clothing, sitting as we were without the shelter of a creek. Our hands and guns grew drier though, which was a help.

I checked up on my cartridge belt, and cursed softly. Carelessly I'd filled a dozen gaps with ordinary shells instead of William's lacquered ones, and these were now swollen beyond redemption, their paper cases worn half through where they'd rubbed against my jacket. The lacquer on the others was cracked in places, but they all slipped in and out the chambers easily enough. It was the first proof I'd encountered of that particular pudding, and with a full dry bag alongside for replacements I felt I'd got off lightly.

Gradually the daylight went. No warning colours, no slowly sinking sun, just clouds that thickened and grew heavier. Great rafts of gulls came drifting high and wing set out towards the mud; and passing them, two perfect, swifter Vs of curlew. A pair of redshanks tried to come in to the flash, saw us and twisted violently aside with an indignant "lee—leu—leu" of protest and warning. Presently a lone black-headed gull beat low and wearily across the saltings to light with a faint plop on the near side of the pool. As he flapped rather wildly to retain his balance I saw that one leg stuck out stiff and useless, and the flank above was dark with clotted blood. Some adolescent criminal had been diverting himself in the name of sport, and this was the result.

For a full minute the gull stood watching us quite fearlessly; then took off with a small cry and beat laboriously on out to sea.

"Poor devil. He'll be lucky to see the spring," William said bitterly.

So flight time passed, and the greyness even in the west grew dark. We hadn't seen a single duck, and not even a curlew had passed in range of us. Away to the left the lights of the town were throwing their reflection on the low cloud-ceiling, and I thought of the fairgoers I had met last night. Tonight, perhaps, they had the laugh on me.

"Time we shifted a little," said William, getting to his feet and stretching.

Then, in the short space as I stirred to follow, came a swift splash from in front, and, an instant later, the sibilance of wildly thrashing wings. For a second I saw a small black shadow rising swiftly, and in that second fired, and Bill leaped forward.

"Well done, indeed," came from the darkness, and I purred softly to myself. Then as I joined William—

"Look what Bill's brought me," and he passed the body. It was a duck all right—my first qualm passed. At least it was coloured dark and light and widgeon-sized; the beak seemed queerly large. Then I knew I was holding a drake shoveller, the first I'd ever shot. More than ever I regretted William's ban on torches (he swore they lost more duck than ever they found at night) for I did so want to see that lovely plumage. Carefully I laid him down on a clump of vegetation so that he should not get soiled.

It was then, and only then, that I realized William's strategy. No widgeon had come at flight time, which was all that I'd considered with that sky. But now we moved round to face inland, with the flash between us and the town, and fair lights reflected in the sky.

It was the very depth and thickness of the clouds I'd cursed that made the whole scheme possible—that and the lucky chance of fair week to provide the extra glare.

William was busy twenty yards away collecting a pile of crab-grass for Bill. When he came back to sit alongside me I noticed that he'd shed his coat.

"Dog's a dam nuisance at this game when he shivers and licks himself all the time; can't listen properly," he grumbled, half to himself. Then more cheerfully, "With a flash as small as this we'd better take alternate first shots. You lead off. Likely we'll have an hour's wait at least before much happens, though."

We had, and more. I watched the hands of my watch move slowly round to half-past five, then six, then six-fifteen. There was plenty of time to study the possibilities in front.

That belt of lit-up sky seemed pretty narrow, when you came to look at it. Above it the clouds hung dark as pitch, and against the loom of the land beneath no duck would show. Closer again, the water threw back a little of the sky's reflection. I rather thought my money would be on the widgeon, even supposing they did come.

Six-thirty—then alone and unheralded the first bird arrived. He just slipped quietly in, tearing the water's surface into widening ripples as he pitched. For the life of me I couldn't pick him out; there seemed to be at least a dozen blobs out there I hadn't seen before. Another splash, and he was gone. I heard his wing-beats, and that was all.

"I never saw him either." William must have overheard my muttered maledictions.

Another quarter of an hour passed and then, to no uncertain tune, those widgeon started moving.

One moment, silence—the feeling silence of a lonely salting on a dark and moonless night. A whistle—wings. More wings and whistling—and kurring everywhere.

Lord, but they were mad moments that followed. Black silhouettes, appearing from nowhere, teetering for an instant against that belt of lighter darkness, then dropping downward out of sight. Sometimes they showed for another second as they flared, but by no means always. If we missed them in that second as they hovered, the widgeon won.

I found that if I knelt my line of vision was too high. Birds dropped too fast across the only spot where they were visible. The only hope was to catch them against it as they checked to pitch. That wasn't easy, either. Sitting on the flat ground I found it best to follow the principle of the lying pit—legs pointing roughly forty-five degrees to the right of where you hope to shoot. At least I found I tied myself in simpler knots that way than in any other.

The whole performance was crazily unorthodox but wildly thrilling. Concentration keyed up to tiptoe point—ears strained to catch the calling or the swish of wings; eyes restless, yet intent on that small strip of cloud, every muscle tensed to answer automatically.

Widgeon were calling—William answering. Black shapes a-flicker—the old gun's leap; Bill splashing forward to collect—or not. More often not.

Time ceased to be. I might have been there minutes or all night. Widgeon kept coming; the darkness was living to their rush of music.

Then, suddenly it seemed, there were no widgeon. For a long while there was silence. A singleton slipped in—defeated us—and went. The tempo of the night slowed imperceptibly. I shivered, then realized I was soaking wet and chilled to the bone, and rain was falling once again. A glance at my watch showed nine o'clock, and my cartridge bag felt very light, and rattled.

"Finis," came William's voice, and we set about stowing away the spoils.

"We may live a long time and never see a night like this again," he added quietly.

It was nearly eleven when at length we reached the cottage; although, as I didn't fail to emphasize, we'd have been back an hour earlier if we had only taken a torch. It took at least that time to discover where Bill had dragged his master's coat as he set off after the first of the nine-and-twenty widgeon he had gathered.

21

February 19—i

That February continued to live up to its name, for rain fell steadily all the following week, and the wireless and newspapers daily spoke of threatened floods. With the moon's change, however, the weather improved. We had the conventional three days of white frost and then, instead of rain came wind.

A strong breeze was blowing in my teeth as I pedalled from the station on Friday night. It was sad to think of this as the last of the shooting season; but, as the thrills of that last incredible week-end still dazzled on my brain, there seemed no limit to the possibilities the saltings—or William—might be holding for me over the next two days. But William wasn't quite so wildly hopeful. "I've no particular ideas on how we're going to spend our time, Rory," he told me. "Truth is I've been too busy to do much reconnoitring since you left, and I reckon the old Army saying about time spent in reconnaissance being seldom wasted applies to this coastal game more than any other form of shooting! I'll be busy tomorrow, too, worse luck.

Tell you what, though—" he went on thoughtfully, "You're beginning to know the ropes a little. I'll give you what gleanings I've gathered since last time; the car's very much at your service and you can produce a plan of campaign for us.

"To begin with, I tried three more nights after those widgeon of ours without really getting among them again. Despite the rain the flashes were shrinking, and although the tide'll have flooded them again two or three nights ago, there's been no rain since. On t'other hand I don't think the widgeon have gone, as I was talking to one of the trawler skippers only Wednesday and he told me he'd seen more duck—widgeon and mallard—out to sea this past fortnight than all the season, and Amos doesn't usually exaggerate. If they're feeding inland there may be a few on this fen; about the only other bet is if they're way out on the mud, where there are one or two beds of that skinny type of zostera—I believe the botanists call it nana as opposed to the usual marina.

"I also did one morning flight over at Seton while the moon was still setting, well before daybreak, when I should think the best part of a thousand geese came in. But they're an uncertain quantity just now when they're thinking of collecting for migration. You might go down to morrow and find five thousand there—or just as likely not a bird.

"The only other tit-bit of information I've got for you is that for the last few evenings I've been hearing several odd snipe scraping around at dusk. For the first week in March last year with conditions much as now, there was a big lot down on the fen, and Harry and I were cursing impotently! Only if you do go down, please don't shoot a mallard. It's a pet foible of mine that no inland mallard—or woodcock—should be shot after the end of January. I b'lieve we'd find our home-bred stock increasing quite a bit if no one did. But that's by the way. I've talked quite enough nonsense for one evening, and I'll trouble you to give that jug of beer a fair wind. Thanks."

And William subsided into a series of contented gurgles. Nor could I gather any further information out of him.

I lay awake some time that night weighing up the pros and cons of the morrow's entertainment.

Geese—or widgeon?

Assuming both were in, what help could we look for from the elements? Moonrise at least three hours after dark, high water not so very far behind, and a wind, if it held, that was blowing straight out from the land. This time of the year the widgeon would be out to sea by day and coming in well after dark to feed; and we didn't know where. William had more than hinted that the flashes were too dry. They might get on to the zos beds before the sea covered them, but, quite apart from the darkness, we couldn't, as the creeks would fill up first. If they chose, they could ride the tide till the beds were again uncovered, or come in with it to guzzle among the salting grasses as it lapped them. Either course seemed eminently safe. If they were feeding inland they were out of court in any case—unless there were any down on William's fen. I'd have to do a scout around tomorrow. Even the problematical wind didn't appear to hold out much hope unless it blew strongly during the day and made them so uncomfortable on the mudbanks that they flighted in early with the mallard.

No, all in all to my mind those widgeon didn't appear to offer a very rosy proposition.

And the geese? Well, I thought they'd be feeding in land by day, and with at least three hours of darkness between dusk and moonrise would almost certainly come out for sand or sleep. The tide might shift them a bit—it could certainly cover their roosting bars—and they'd have to flight again some time between moonrise and morning depending largely on the quality of the light. Also, if the wind held, they'd be flighting back straight into it.

On the face of it the elements seemed to point quite firmly towards trying for a goose, though how to find where and if there were any geese to try for?

But of course, at evening flight I'd see not only the direction they came from but also on which sand bars they were roosting! I might even see a mallard, too. Overcome by the brilliance of my reasoning I rocked happily off to sleep.

Over breakfast I told William I'd like to wander round the fen in the morning and borrow the car in the afternoon.

"I'll be back for dinner at seven," I added, as casually as I knew how. William appeared unimpressed. He was smiling a little as he scribbled a few words on a scrap of paper, which he proceeded to fold carefully and then slip under the clock on the mantelpiece.

"You're the general," was his only comment.

After a decent interval I filled my belt with number eights and went with Harry to investigate the "snipe-pit".

I took up my position straight up-wind of it, ten yards behind a tall thick hawthorn hedge. I could see Harry climb the gate into the far end of the field, and almost immediately through the bare black twigs I caught a white flicker as the first bird jumped. Swinging and darting, he came low and straight for me. Then lifted to clear the fence and, as the wind took him, went on lifting. A second bird was with him, and did the same. There were four birds there, two right and lefts; for they came just beautifully. One, two—ten seconds' pause—three, four.

I'd like to know how far beneath those first three birds my shot-strings passed. The fourth was out of luck, and spun down and back to land in the very top of the highest and thickest hawthorn in all that thick high fence.

Over the next few minutes I prefer to draw a veil. The snipe was not the only thing that bled.

I sent Harry back then. The fen was large, maybe three miles by one without a stitch of cover for any sort of drive, and I thought maybe one wandering body might get by where two would serve no useful purpose and only be the more conspicuous. At that I was not so wise, for Harry knew the fen and I did not, and that fen was cut up into individual fields by dykes instead of fences—dykes which at the present water level were not only stock but human proof save where occasional half-sunken planks made "bridges". Sometimes there were gateways, but more often not, and seldom indeed in the corners where I wanted them!

I have a predilection, no more, for walking my snipe down wind wherever possible, but I soon found myself involved in a web of waterways, the intricacies of which would have made the Hampton Court Maze look silly.

However, I persevered. The saving grace was that the snipe were in, and by no means in the meagre quantities we'd met on previous occasions. From one small field alone I must have flushed two hundred snipe—too wild to fire a single shot. Wisp after wisp of grey-white flinders that jack-in-a-boxed out of the withered grass to a chorus of protesting screaks; twisting low away for a hundred yards so that their brown-streaked backs merged almost invisibly into the brown-streaked herbage, then zooming steeply, till the dull sky was criss-crossed with individual bat shapes, each weaving erratically its independent course.

It was curious how some fields appealed to them, while others to all appearances equally succulent, with equal cover and equally squishy after the rain, held none—or at most a singleton tucked away in a corner. William had told me, I remembered; but it was quite another matter to see it for myself! It wasn't as if they hadn't visited the other fields, either, for I found old cow-pats in almost every one that were beak-bored until they looked like colanders. Yet five fields each produced wisps totalling considerably over a hundred snipe, while from the thirty or forty others I tramped I doubt if I flushed above a scattered score in all.

All the same, it was the stray singletons that helped my pocket far more than the big wisps. All but two of the dozen shots I had were at odd out-fliers, and even they, with the aid of the stiffish south-west wind that swept unchecked across the fen, didn't linger over their departure. Usually when I was least expecting it came that half heard frrp! and, if I was lucky enough to have the wind at my back at the moment, the split-second flick of white and dainty pencilled underwing as a snipe bellied into the breeze before it turned to twist away before it. There was little chance for laggard shooting.

It was very noticeable how that flick of white served to focus the eye quickly. Alone, and quartering the ground, it was inevitable that I should flush some birds up-wind of me. I don't think on the average these got up any closer or any wilder than the rest, but they stole away hugging the ground and started twisting sooner; more important Still on a dull winter's day, without that warning flash of white I found them almost unconscionably hard to pick up quickly against a background that repeated to such a large degree the colours of their upper plumage.

It was a keen and happy morning altogether. Each patch of rushes, tuft of grass might spin into the air its darting flinder. Twice I met larks—and very nearly fell from grace!

Most fields held traces of the recent floods, and all of these I scanned most carefully, breathlessly listening at every step lest a snipe should jump while my eyes were otherwise engaged. Unfairly enough, my gumboots in such places made the most deceptive snipe-like noises!

Twice I found signs of widgeon. Not much, but had I had the

time either spot might have been worth a nighttime visit. It wouldn't have meant widgeon only in all probability, for there had been plovers galore playing around every little splash of water that the floods had left behind.

I almost kicked a hare that was lying in one thick patch of rushes. "Big as a calf" she looked as she cantered off across the fen, her hind feet throwing up twin sprays at every splash she crossed. I envied her knowledge of where the "liggers" lay across the dykes, for she made full use of them on her way back to the plough.

I glanced at my watch—then shook it foolishly, and looked at it again, but the hands still showed half-past one. With a slightly sinking feeling I remembered lunch had been at one, and here I was two miles away beleagured in a maze of dykes! I knew time wouldn't worry William overmuch, but this afternoon I had other fish to fry. More over, if this wind held there seemed a chance that they might come into the pan.

My best route for a speedy return seemed to lie along the riverbank. To achieve it would entail going a bit out of my way, but once there at least I would not have to search for liggers every hundred yards. Ten minutes later I was clambering on to it.

Qu—a—ack!

Perhaps for a second we eyed each other. Not three feet from the bank, and straight below my feet, a mallard drake was gently paddling against the stream.

The unexpectedness, the sheer perfection of that glimpse just held me spellbound. There wasn't a feather out of place; each point of plumage; fresh tailored and fresh groomed for the spring of the year.

The burnished head, its small bright eye cocked up at me enquiringly; the grey and brown and black streaked back tapering to a jaunty tight black curl above his tail; the ripple of water parting round that gleaming chestnut breast—a picture wholly and utterly instinct with life, and glowing with the vitality of perfect health. Surely he couldn't realize that his death lay in the tubes I carried, for I will swear he showed no fear at all.

For a full second he gazed at me quite calmly. Then with a splash the bubble burst and the ripples widened as a sprinkling of drops fell back among them. And from the bank beneath me came another splash, then another, and another—six ducks who jumped and beat away in a welter of wildly thrashing wings that scattered drops of water as they fled.

Before they were even out of range the welter had resolved into three clear pairs. Three mallards and their wives, who still held together just for company.

I stood gazing open-mouthed and rapt as any zany till they had grown quite small.

They'd provided such a lovely ending to a memorable morning—the thought crossed my mind that I was glad it hadn't all happened two months ago; the ending would have been so very different. And that, in me, was a queer thought.

22

February 19—ii

It was close on two hours later that I pulled the old bus to a gently scrunching stop just back of a sea was nearly thirty miles away, with still a couple more to walk along before I reached the spot I had in mind.

This evening I wasn't really out for blood. Here was where William had seen his thousand geese last week, and my object now was twofold. Firstly to find out if they were still here. Then, if they were, to note exactly where they crossed the sea wall on their journey out to roost, and if possible what banks they chose to roost on.

It was a nice dry occupation for the coast. I simply snuggled into the sea wall nicely out of the wind, lit a pipe and gave myself up to contemplation of the saltings; albeit with an ear well cocked for any noises inland.

The wind was blowing steadily from behind me. Nothing very startling in the way of winds, but quite enough to grumble as the twisted branches of the odd elms and willows growing along inside the sea wall raked it. I moved a little to get well clear of the trees and keep my ears free of the moaning.

The sky was passable. The clouds were thick, certainly, but they were high and moving pretty rapidly, and it seemed at least a fair bet that at that rate of progress there'd be some change in their consistency ere morning.

Low over the sea wall to the east I caught a stir of movement. A little bunch of birds, sharp-winged and swift, were dipping down to skim the saltings.

Shank? Knots? Goldies?

Golden plover they were. I saw them clearly as they rose again, and they were swinging round towards me as I cowered.

Lord, but those birds were moving! Fifty or sixty of them racing straight down the saltings; rising in unison again, as a flock of dunlin sometimes will, to hurl them selves downward in a silver shower for the sheer wild joy of movement.

A hundred yards outside me they passed to a refrain of clear sweet pipes, then angled in to cross the sea wall to my left. They made a pretty sight, but I wished they'd passed a few yards closer in!

I was watching a miscellaneous collection of waders out on the edge of the mud and thinking longingly of William's glasses when I heard a tiny rustle in the grass alongside.

A thimbleful of soft brown fur appeared, which scrabbled up my thigh boot and boldly scampered down the length of this new highway to sit up calmly on my ankle and resolve itself into a short-tailed field vole. For a moment it eyed me entirely unconcerned, and then, if you please, proceeded to wash its face and ears!—licking its tiny forepaws and rubbing them round exactly as Madam Pussy does on the mat before the fire.

When it had finished—and not, I am certain, one minute before—it huffed itself up, and shook itself, and then hopped lightly down to begin rummaging fussily among the jetsam of some old high-water mark for its supper.

The delightful effrontery of the whole performance was quite absorbing. I never even noticed it was growing dark till I was abruptly recalled to business by the very sound I'd come all this way to hear.

Faint at first and distant, dropping down the wind, but unmistakably the cry of geese. They didn't sound a big lot. Then

I saw them, and for a moment almost disbelieved my eyes. The leading skein alone must have spanned above a quarter of a mile of salting, and behind it came another and another—a tangle of lesser skeins stretched back until the last ones faded. No, they weren't talking—much.

High, and astonishingly fast, they rode the wind right out to sea, while I strained my eyes to follow.

Surely they were lowering—or was it just the horizon coming up to meet them? No, for they were hues no longer. A small dark cloud that gently lowered and vanished into the endless mud.

How many were there? I hadn't the least idea. Only that there were many times the thousand William had spoken of.

Marks? Yes, they must have come out about over that angle in the sea wall half a mile beyond me. Straight down the wind and out; if it held, they should come straight back into it.

Only lower, pray Allah—so much, much lower.

I saw a fair few duck at flight time. They came in early, too, while it was still well daylight. Wedges and strings of mallard, clotted against the darkening clouds. But those that passed near over me were high. As usual some of the more distant ones looked lower, but I rather wondered if it were not just sour grapes.

There seemed to be a tendency even among these coastal Vs to fly by pairs—a reminder that the season was all but over, and the tight sexless companies of winter were loosening at the thought of summer nesting grounds and families.

As I tramped back to the car I thought of the astounding numbers of the fowl I'd seen and marvelled yet again at the excitement of the living pictures which these "lifeless" saltings could produce.

23

February 19—iii

"Over eastern districts strong south to south-westerly winds reaching gale force locally tonight."

Those were the first words I heard as I clumped into the sitting-room, and William reached to turn the wireless down. If I'd needed anything to make me even more excited over tonight's prospects here it was. What a perfectly splendid body the B.B.C. must be—I felt that perhaps I'd never fully appreciated them until this moment!

"Come on, Rory—out with it! And stop looking like the cat that swallowed the canary."

William rudely interrupted my beatific visions of swarms of geese fighting in head-high towards me.

So I told him what I'd done—and seen.

"Great minds …" he chuckled, handing me the slip of paper from beneath the clock on which I read "Moonrise nine-thirty; prospect at S. for geese at dusk."

Not that I really needed much confirmation, but it seemed a happy omen. So did the dinner we presently sat down to, for it was William's goose from the last time I was down.

As a matter of fact, I'd given a party with mine as the pièce de résistance only two nights before and, apart from the fun of devouring my first wild goose, had not been much impressed by the result which had been rather dry, and rather tough, and with a definite "salty" taste about it.

Not so the bird we tackled now, which was juicy and quite delicious.

"It's all a matter of cooking," William told me, "and Mrs. T. is a wizard on almost any form of game. Wild geese carry surprisingly little fat and to treat 'em as a tame goose in the oven is fatal. Cook 'em well wrapped in bacon —preferably in one of those covered tin affairs that drip—and don't leave 'em in too long. As for the salty taste—shove a raw onion or a chunk or two of charcoal in their tums as you would with a widgeon, and it'll take all that away. Then instead of a cocktail take a ten miles walk along the saltings and miss out on your tea—and you'll wonder how you ever came to think a goose was even a fair-sized bird!"

Well, I'd had a bit of William's cocktail and by the time we'd finished with it that goose did look a shade unsatisfactory.

A little over an hour later we were stepping from the car, adjusting belts and thigh boots, slinging game bags and uncasing guns—going through all the normal rather thrilling motions anticipatory to a period on the saltings. I know that I at least would have needed very little provocation to caper like a puppy in the snow!

It was suddenly very dark as William snapped the lights off. For a minute we stood quite still to allow our eyes to grow accustomed to the change. Then we were off the road, across a dyke and stumbling among the grass tufts on the side of the sea bank itself.

It was a very different pilgrimage from the one I'd made this afternoon. The wind was undoubtedly far stronger—it had made the old bus lurch and hiccup as it struck her on the way along—and now, as we topped the sea wall, we found ourselves leaning quite steeply into it to progress at all. It had moved more southerly, too. Instead of coming broadside from our right, we were definitely edging into it.

Here was another problem. Those geese had pitched a long mile out beyond the saltings and I'd no idea how far inland they had been feeding. Would they jump and fly straight into the wind enough to let them angle down to their feeding grounds? Or would they try to fly straight in, be carried sideways, and make up their leeway swinging into pitch? Even if they were still where I had seen them on the mud, the alteration in the wind was quite enough to change their flight line a mile in either direction!

"Of course, I have known 'em come in on the tide when there's a bit of a wind and sit just off the edge of the saltings," William added to my mental confusion. "But if they have, with any luck we'll hear them there before they jump."

Finally we decided to split up half a mile either side of where they'd crossed the sea wall on their journey out, and to run towards the line the first lot coming in should take. We flipped a coin. William dropped back and I went marching on.

Already it seemed to me there was a lighter darkness over towards the east, and twice I half thought I got a glimpse of stars. For all that, it was plenty dark enough.

To begin with at least, I planned on a "dry" flight, so sat down luxuriously among the debris of the last big tides in lee of the sea wall. Back here, too, where there were no creeks to stumble through or into, I felt so infinitely more mobile in case the geese should start to come in right or left and, in addition to the comfort, I could hear better cut off from the worst lash of the wind.

There is a wonderful feeling of aloneness sitting in the dark on a bare expanse of salting.

You are so very tiny in that bleak infinity that reaches all ways out into the night. Queer thoughts come flooding, enchanting and often silly thoughts that would never dare in the busy light of day, and you have all the time there is to think them out. Small sounds that would pass unheard beneath the sun assume a new importance with the night —the whispering march of the wind among the grasses, the gentle rustle as two dried weed stalks stroke together, the thin high squeak of a foraging shrew above you on the sea wall or the tiny tinkle as a pool drip-drips into the creek that drains it. These and a million other sounds that go to make up the silence of the night.

Then gradually the moon comes pushing up and details on the saltings start to take on concrete shape.

At my feet a streak of lighter darkness along the foot of the sea wall slowly grew into the surface of a muddy track, poached by the sheep flocks herded to and from their daily grazing on the short salt grass. A little farther appeared the leaden surface of a tiny pool, with dark clumps of crab grass overhanging.

That darker line that had meandered nearly up to the sea wall came to be more crab grass fringing on a creeklet. Over years past the lesser tides that had brimmed that creek or lipped a little over, had left along its banks the debris they had brought up with them; among it the floating sage leaves that contained the seeds which presently had taken root.

So gradually came moonrise, though the racing clouds strove hard to hide the fact. Unless they thinned a good deal it would be some time before there was light enough to tempt the geese to move. Still and all, there was the whole night ahead. They'd have to come in some time, and just when it seemed singularly immaterial.

But—was it? I remembered the tide would have turned half an hour since. A suspicion suddenly reared its ugly head that the wind was dropping with the tide.

Once raised, that suspicion proved a brute to lull again. I could still hear the wind swish and rattle among the stunted willows and the deeper thrum as it played with the stiff old branches of the elms. There was still the drive and rustle of its gusts along the grass tops; and when I climbed the wall to listen further it caught me a buffet that fairly made me lean to hold my balance.

Nevertheless I wasn't wholly comforted. The song seemed a thought more puffy, less easily sustained than earlier in the night. I listened avidly, trying to convince myself—and listening, could have sworn I heard a goose speak—once.

One single note, quite clear.

I rushed down the bank again, hoping that out of the wind I should hear more easily, and staring wildly— To have been audible at all that bird must have been quite close.

But minutes drifted by, and gradually the clutch on my gun relaxed—they must have passed by now if they were coming in. Almost I convinced myself that my ears had tricked me. The creaking of a tree—?

And then it came again. Same sound, same place, and the direction was from the saltings straight ahead.

Aankh! One clear sharp note. Some geese—or at the very least one goose—must have shifted in before the tide and pitched on the salts within a few hundred yards of where I sat, a half-way house until the moon should light them in to feed.

The burning question was: how many were there? If the whole lot had moved (even the possibility of all that mass of geese sitting all unsuspecting within a quarter of a mile made me breathe a little short) I'd do better not to disturb them. It'd be any odds that with such a short way to fly they'd give one or t'other of us at least one killable chance when they did decide to jump.

On the other hand, if it was only a small lot, I'd be a fool to miss the chance of a stalk. William had told me that provided you could pinpoint them exactly, it wasn't too hard to belly-crawl up to geese on a dark night among the crab grass on the salting, while if you could find a creek to help—well—

The operative phrase was, of course, "pinpoint them exactly"!

I made a pointer with a bit of driftwood towards where I'd heard the call, and twice within the next half hour it came again. Just the one note. I decided that even if it wasn't a singleton there probably weren't a big lot there.

So presently I started off to make a detour to the left and thus come up across the wind with my objective between me and the lighter east. Which in theory was wonderful. Only it's not so easy on a real dark night to know firstly how far you are out from the sea wall, and therefore when to turn in towards the moon; or secondly when to take to hands and knees and finally to tummy for the last stages of the crawl, when your objective obstinately persists in remaining silent as the tomb and so forces you back on your already more than doubtful calculations as to when that last stage is due.

After all, it is discouraging as well as damping to perform a beautiful stealthy wriggle through some hundred of yards of obscurity, and then, pausing for a breath, to be compelled to admit that you haven't a clue whether your goose is twenty or two hundred yards ahead, to one side or the other, or even if you've snaked right past him in your ardour. Not to mention a growing certainty that he must, under cover of your panting, have departed quietly into the night.

Hot, wet and dishevelled, I was beginning to feel that there was more in this night stalking business than met the eye, when I suddenly found a void beneath my chin and a blessed creek, which at least offered me a chance to crouch and get my breath back in comparative comfort. For the moment I was completely out of touch. The next move was indubitably with the geese.

Ten minutes—a quarter of an hour ticked slowly by. The wind was dropping, too, no doubt of that by now. Its steady drive was sinking into little rushes, and in the lulls between the crab grass silhouettes stood stiff and still. The clouds were thinning too, and then I heard it, quite absurdly close. A call followed by a low-pitched muttering just off to my left, along the line my creek took! They couldn't be a hundred yards away. And they were geese, not goose.

Oh Lord, the odds were with me now. I should get into them.

The sucking slither of my boots against the creek side sounded agonizingly loud. Oh, quietly—take care—you idiot, you've got all night.

Some fifty yards I covered bent in two, while the geese kept ominously silent. Then straightened slowly; and as I straightened the moon sailed clear through a window in the cloud and every tuft and all the salting was dipped in a milky light. Surely those geese must show—if they were geese and not mere chimerae? And then I made them out five, six, ten, twenty necks or so, held stiff as ramrods; maybe seventy yards away, and not a dozen from my creek.

Back down and on—and then they jumped!

No, I don't think they'd seen me. It was just that they considered the moon was bright enough for them to move inland. Only alas, they didn't move direct, but angled in across my front.

Oh, Lord, how far off were they? They were so very low.

I hesitated, then in desperation fired and fired again. It wasn't in any way a pretty thing to do. And the geese climbed wildly and presently they shouted their disgust and went on, clamouring, inland.

Hell—hell—hell!

Is there anything like the utter emptiness and misery after you've been close to geese and then in some way failed? For several minutes I sat there just fighting back to equanimity—against the thought "if only".

Presently I rose and stood upright beside the creek. I'd got nearer the salting edge than I'd imagined, for I could see its hard black fringe against the leaden gleam of the tide-wet mud.

I took a step towards it—the whole black fringe went up in

one great roar of wings and in a shouting chorus beat off out to sea. Even before they vanished I saw them stringing into Vs and echelons.

All the geese, all the geese must have come in on the tide and had been sitting there just waiting for the moon. But why my shot had not moved them I could not understand.

In a despair too deep for words I turned and headed back for William.

"They'll likely move again soon, now the moon's come clear," was all he said. "We might as well wait another hour or so and see."

We didn't have to. In less than a quarter of that time their vanguard came driving in. But the wind had dropped, and besides, they'd had their warning.

During the next half hour we each had many geese clear overhead, black limned against the cloud shawls or dim before the stars, and all the time their thrilling heady chorus grew and waned.

In that high music I thought I heard a paean of triumph in the trials and hardships of another winter overcome—the brave song of a joyous homeward journey towards the gay brightness and sunshine of an Arctic summer.

And as I listened, the smart of my defeat first eased, then vanished quite, till I found myself glad with their gladness, and filled with a deep content in their passing.

Auf wiedersehen, you beauties. In October or November I shall be seeing you once more.